CLOCKWORK PLANET
V

STORY BY YUU KAMIYA & TSUBAKI HIMANA
MANGA BY KURO
CHARACTER DESIGN BY SINO

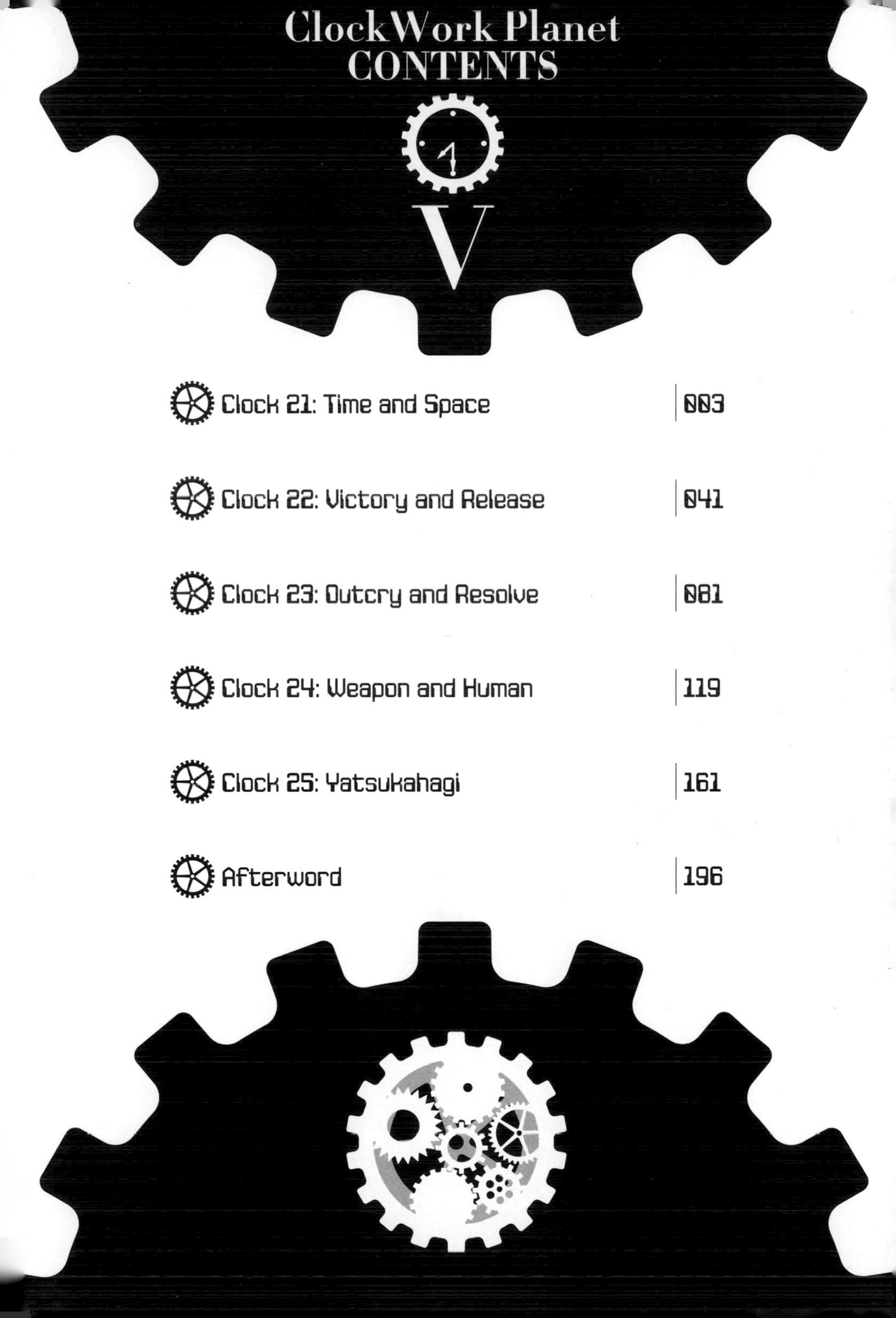

ClockWork Planet CONTENTS

V

DEFINITION DECLARATION: RYUZU THE YOURSLAVE, UNIT I OF THE INITIAL-Y SERIES.
A SOUND SPILLED OUT.
INITIATING SHIFT FROM CLOCK 1, REAL TIME, TO CLOCK 2, IMAGINARY TIME.
ENEMY THREAT: CATEGORY V. INITIATING SHIFT TO DIFFERENCE CHAKRA 12.
DEFINITION DECLARATION: ANCHOR THE TRISHULA, UNIT IV OF THE INITIAL-Y SERIES.
LIKE A VOW OF MATRI-MONY.
LIKE A CRY OF ANGUISH.
THE FINAL VERSES THEY RECITED, THE MOST HERETICAL AND BLAS-PHEMOUS IN THIS WORLD-

MUTE SCREAM

Clock 21: Time and Space
BLOODY MURDER

TICK
SOON AFTER:
TICK
"MUTE SCREAM," RYUZU'S EXCLUSIVE FEATURE...
CON-VERTED "REAL TIME" ...
ZSH
ZWISH

TICK
...INTO "DUAL TIME," WHICH LIMITLESSLY SUSPENDS REALITY.

AT A SPEED WITH WHICH NO ONE IN THE WORLD COULD CATCH HER...
...SHE TRAVELED THE SPACE BETWEEN 0 AND 1 SECOND.
ROAR
BUT...
WAVER

SCRUNCH
ANCHOR ...
REACHED INTO THE GAPS OF TIME AND SPACE...
GRRR

...AND WRENCHED IT OPEN!

NO ONE SHOULD HAVE BEEN ABLE TO EVEN OBSERVE RYUZU'S MOVE- MENTS...
...LET ALONE SEIZE THEM...
OR LEAP OVER THEM.
!
THEN ...

...SHE LOWERED HER GIANT CLAWS TO RIP RYUZU APART, ALONG WITH DUAL TIME ITSELF.

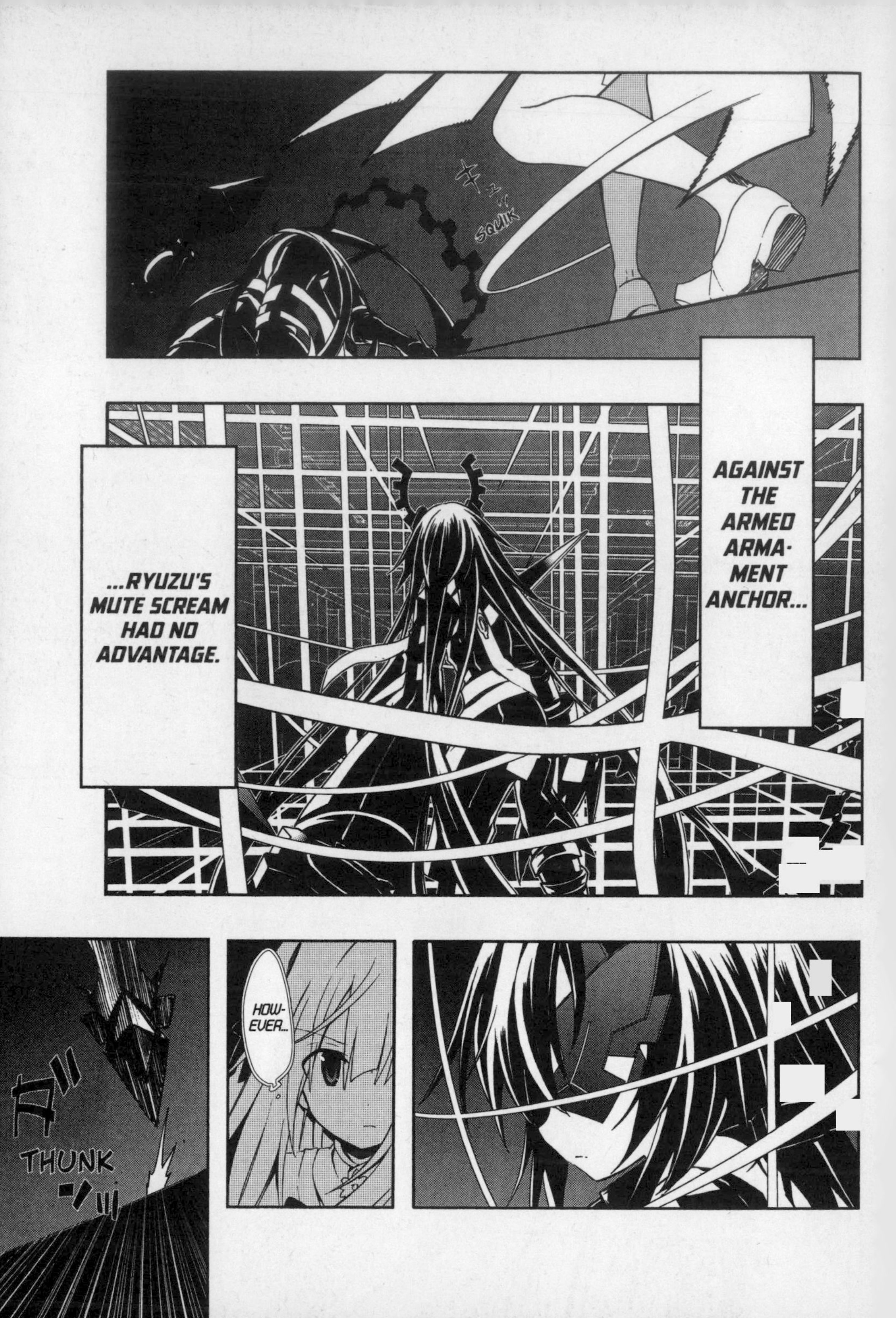

SQUIK
AGAINST THE ARMED ARMAMENT ANCHOR...
...RYUZU'S MUTE SCREAM HAD NO ADVANTAGE.
HOW-EVER...
THUNK

...THAT DOES NOT MEAN THAT I HAVE LOST!
VWOOM
I SHALL PRIORITIZE SPEED...
ROAR
...AND KEEP HER BUSY...
BAM
BAM
BAM
BAM

ス
SST
ウ
BAM
BAM
BAM
BAM
BAM
BAM

RIP
RIP RIP
BOOM

SO...
SHE MUST BE MANIPU-LATING SPACE...
THIS WAS THE PRIMARY FEATURE OF ANCHOR AS A WEAPON.
RRR
WARP
IN SYNCH WITH RYUZU'S SCYTHES, ANCHOR WAS CREATING SMALL DISTORTIONS IN SPACE AND USING THEM AS SHIELDS.
WHOOSH
!
THIS EFFECTIVELY NULLIFIED RYUZU'S ATTACKS.
—LATING SPACE...

AS EX-
PECTED...
...NO,
AS PLANNED.

THREE DAYS EARLIER—
THE PROBABILITY OF MY VICTORY IN A SERIOUS MATCH AGAINST ANCHOR IS ZERO.

HMM... BUT YOU DON'T HAVE TO WIN, YOU KNOW?
YOU JUST HAVE TO BREAK HER.
MASTER NAOTO, IT IS THE SAME THING.

I WAS BORN A SERVANT, AND SHE, A WEAPON.
EVEN WITH YOUR MUTE SCREAM?
YES. SHE WILL MOST LIKELY CATCH UP TO ME USING SHEER FORCE.
THERE IS NO WAY TO COMPENSATE FOR THE DIFFERENCE IN OUR SPECIFI-CATIONS.
THERE'S ONLY ONE THING TO DO, THEN.

USE ME AS A HUMAN SHIELD.
OUT OF THE QUESTION.
...
DO YOU UNDERSTAND WHAT YOU'RE SAYING?

ANCHOR'S CAPTIVITY IS A TRIFLE COMPARED TO THE PROSPECT OF EXPOSING MASTER NAOTO TO DANGER.
IT WAS THE ONE LINE RYUZU COULD EVER CROSS.
IN THAT MOMENT, SHE DIDN'T HAVE A CHOICE, NOR ROOM FOR DOUBT.
THE INFINITE ENERGY COURSING THROUGH ANCHOR'S IMMENSE CLAWS AS THEY SWIPED FORTH CONTINUOUSLY...
ROARRR
...EXCEEDED THE CAPACITY OF SPACE-TIME.
GHK
SO...

...ANCHOR BROKE DOWN COSMIC LAW AND SPED UP FURTHER...
...AND CAUGHT UP TO RYUZU!!

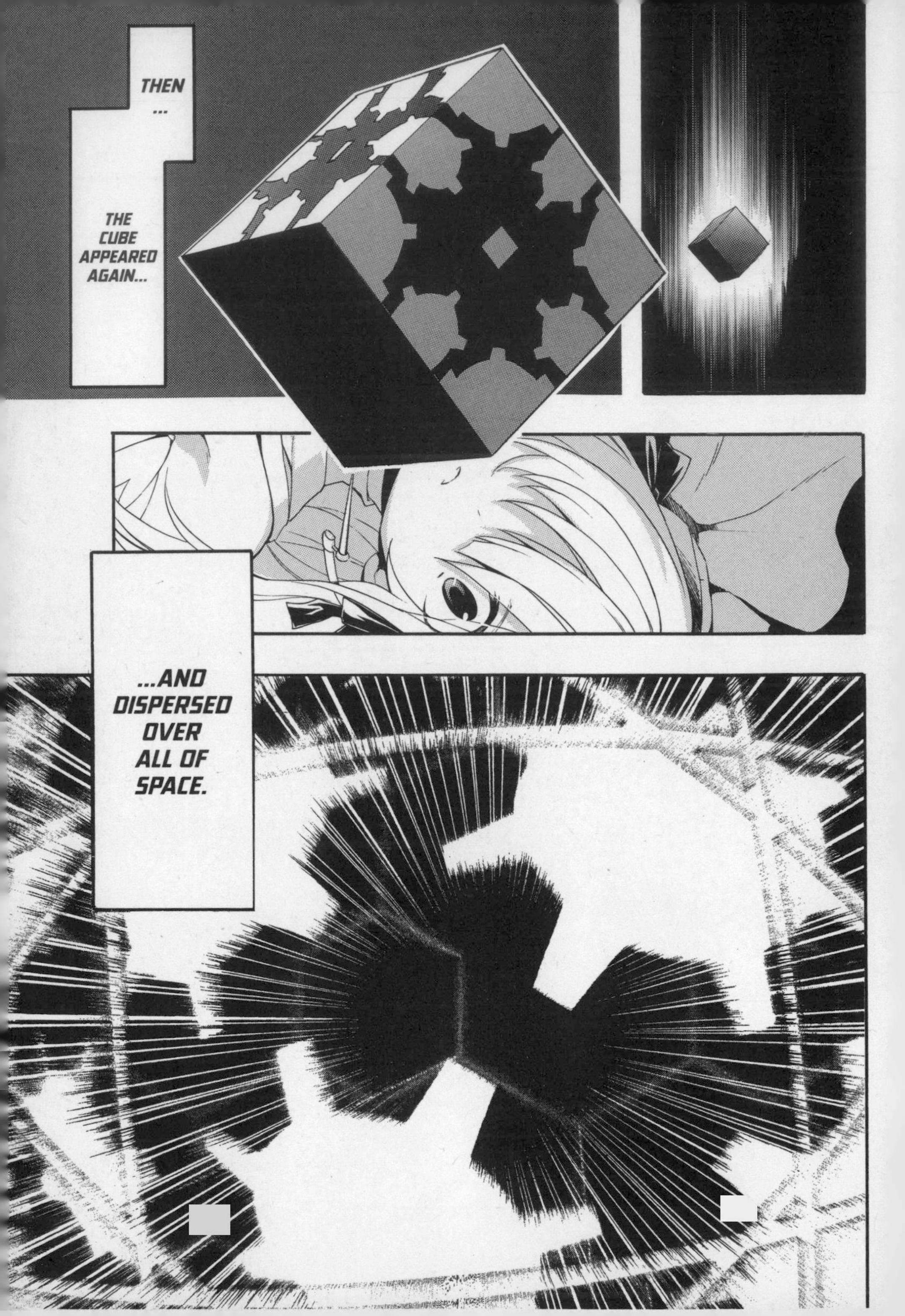
THEN
...
THE CUBE APPEARED AGAIN...
...AND DISPERSED OVER ALL OF SPACE.

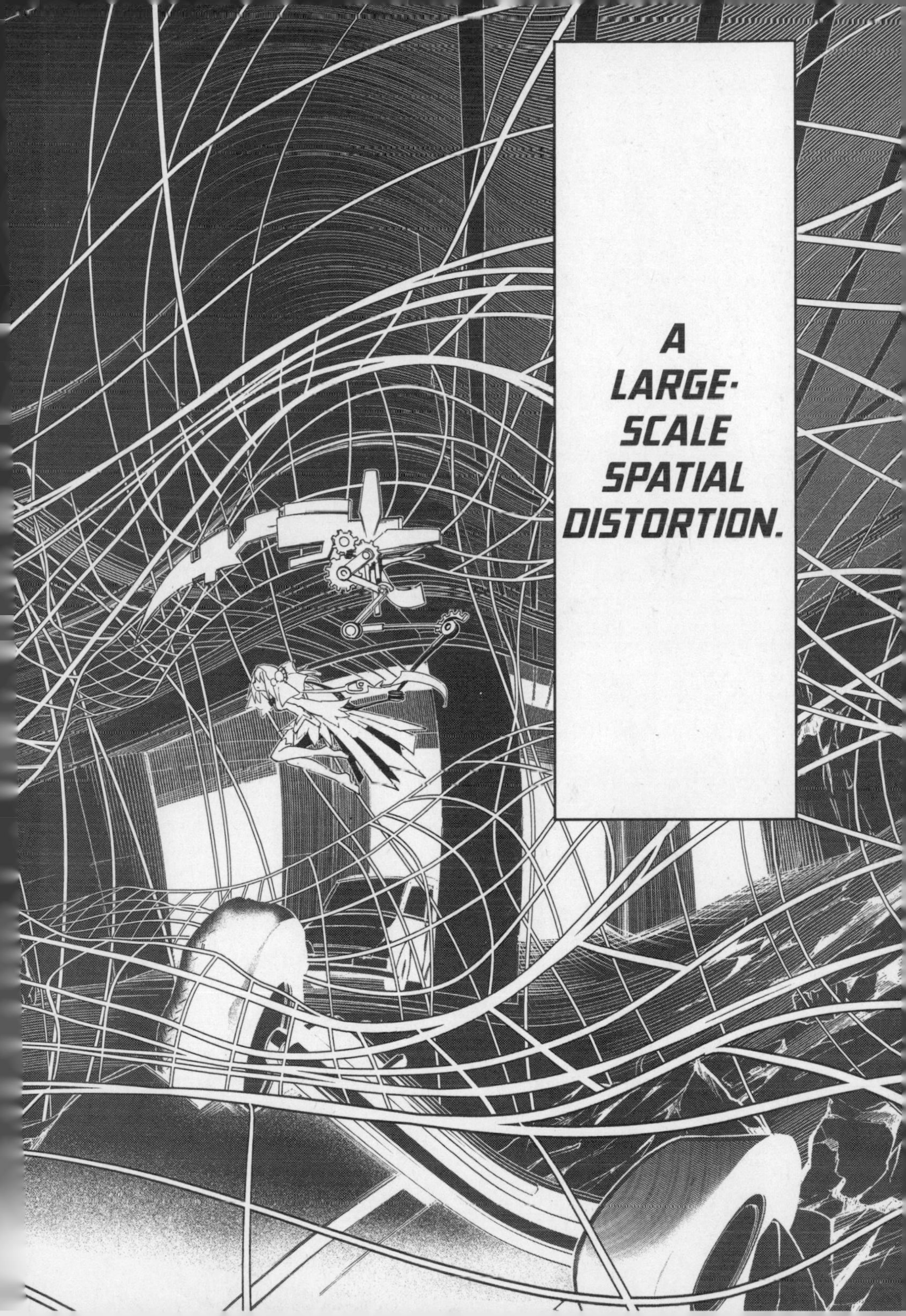
A LARGE-SCALE SPATIAL DISTORTION.

ROAR
A WEB
OF SPACE
RUSHED
UPON HER!

!
SHUNK
GRK
GRK
GRK
ONE OF HER SCYTHES WAS CAUGHT AND CRUMPLED UP, AS IF MADE OF PAPER.
WHIP
WHOOSH
HER BODY WAS THROWN OFF BALANCE ...
...INTO A TAILSPIN.

CRACK

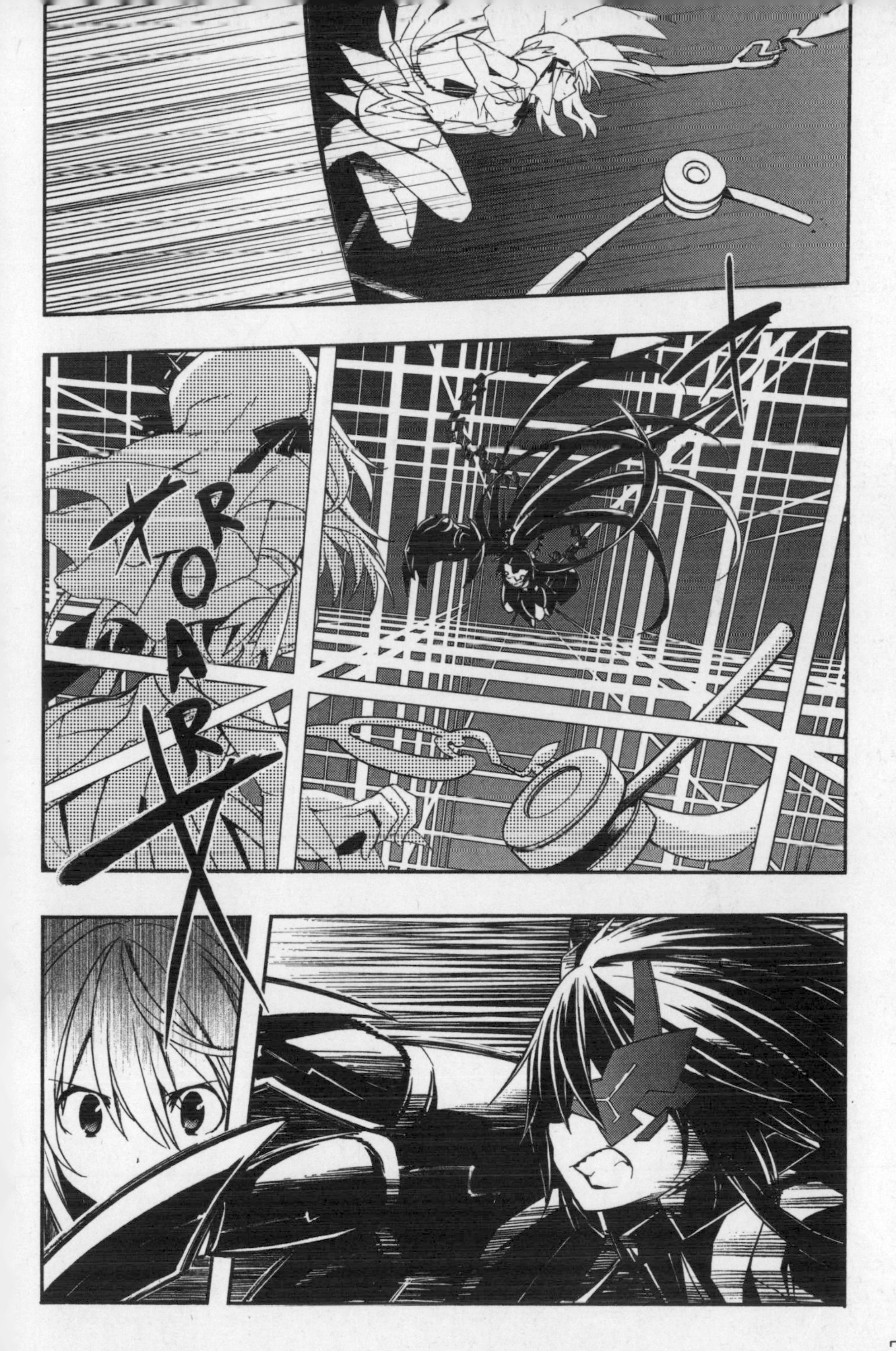
ROAR

MASTER NAOTO.
YOU WANT TO BE A HUMAN SHIELD? DO YOU TRULY HAVE NO CONCERN FOR YOUR OWN LIFE?
HUH? WHAT DO YOU MEAN?
I'LL BET MY LIFE, BUT I SURE DON'T WANT TO LOSE IT.
I'M JUST CONFIDENT WE'RE GOING TO WIN.

I'M NOT GONNA DIE...
...AND ANCHOR'S NOT GONNA KILL ME.
I HAVE LOST ONE OF MY WEAPONS.
MY RATE OF ATTACK HAS BEEN LOWERED— MY OPTIONS HALVED...
HOW- EVER...

...NOW I CAN INCREASE MY SPEED.
THERE ARE NO PROBLEMS HERE.
ANCHOR, I BELIEVE IN YOU.
AND...
MASTER NAOTO...

...I TRUST YOUR WORDS MORE THAN ANYONE ELSE'S. I BELIEVE IN YOU ABOVE ALL.
SO...

I SHALL FLY FASTER,
FASTER,
FASTER,

AND
BETTER!

I KNOW YOU CAN EXECUTE IT WELL.
...MASTER NAOTO, HOW ARE YOU SO SURE THAT YOU WILL NOT BE KILLED BY ANCHOR?
'CAUSE ...

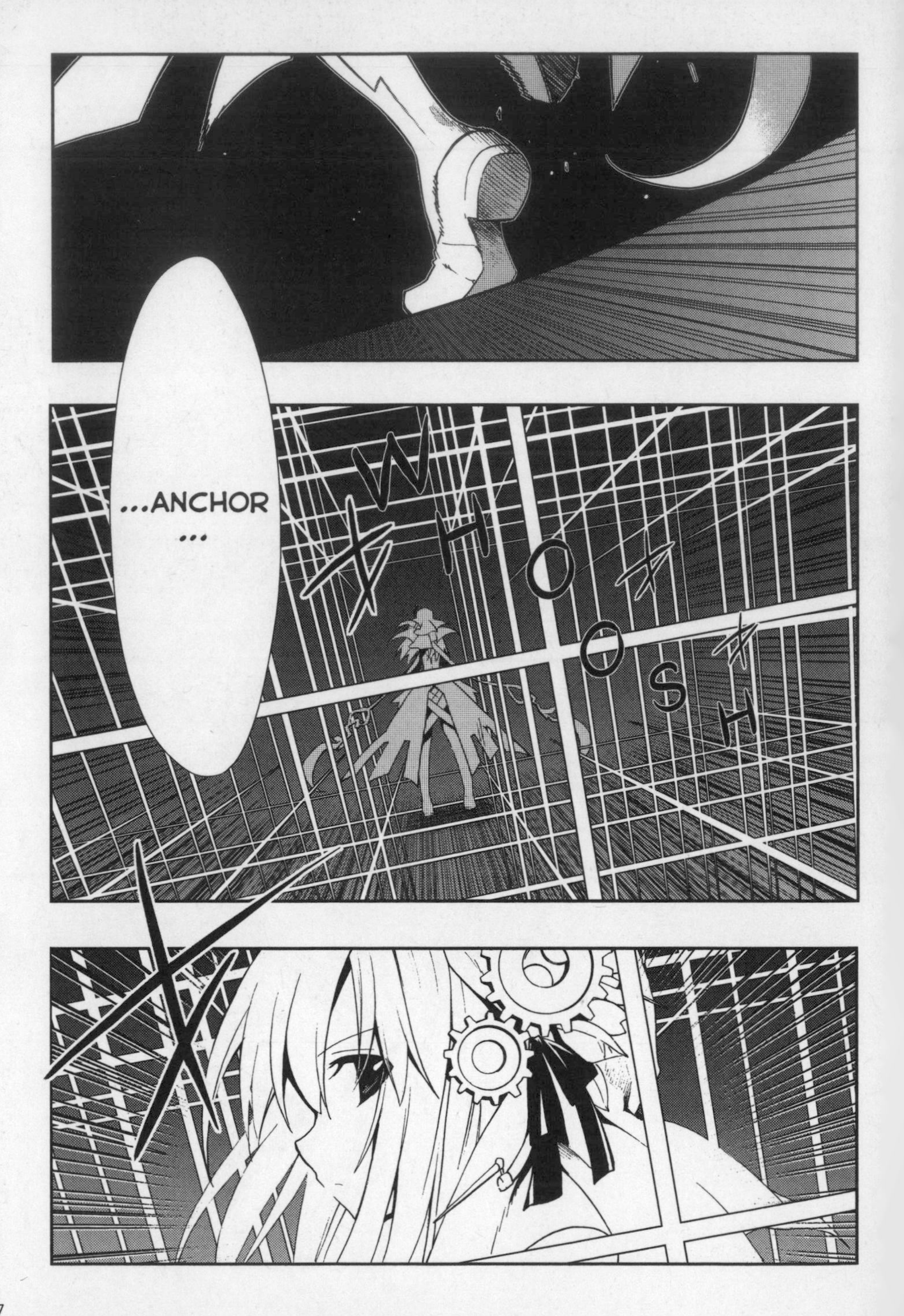
...ANCHOR
...
WHOOSH

...CAN'T
KILL
PEOPLE.

Clockwork
Planet

Clockwork
Planet

Clock 22: Victory and Release

ANCHOR CAN'T KILL PEOPLE.

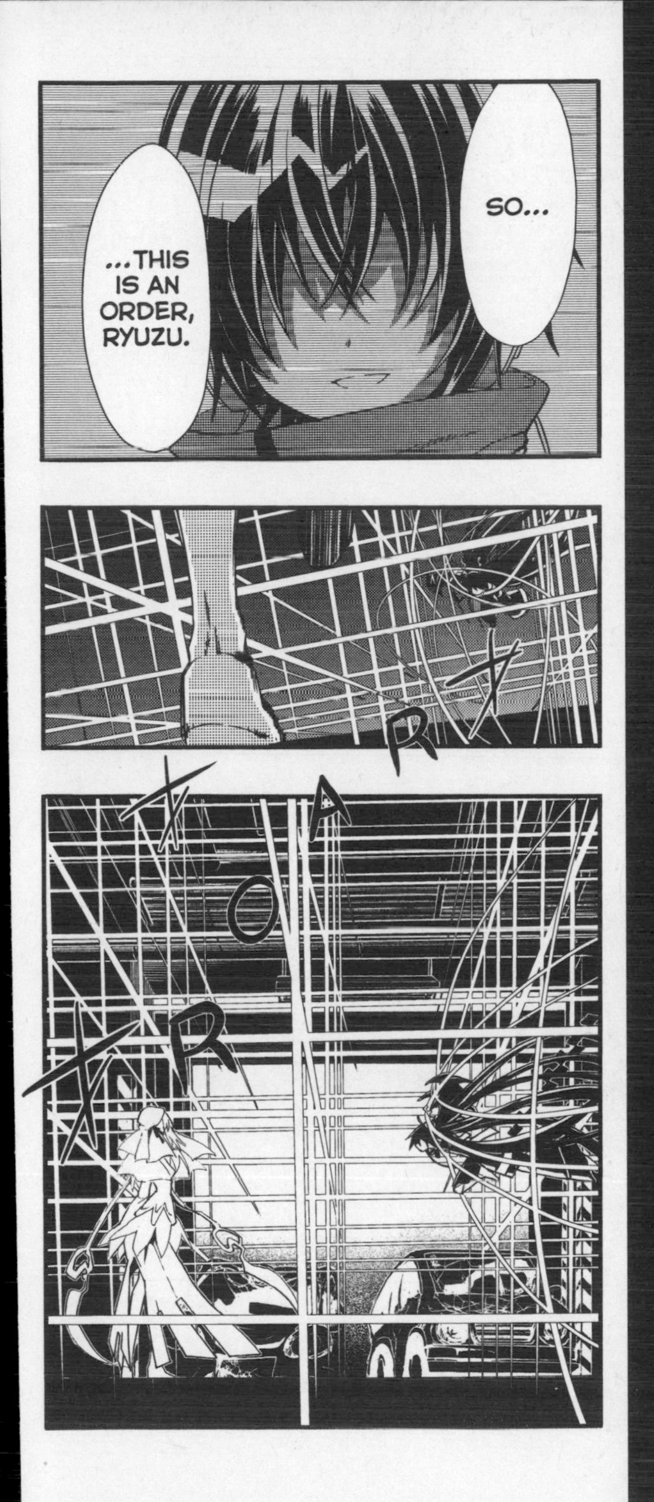

USE ME AS A SHIELD, AND SAVE ANCHOR.
ROAR
FWISH

ピタッ
FREEZE

MAKE ANCHOR VULNERABLE BY USING A HUMAN SHIELD...
IT WORKED JUST AS YOU SAID, MASTER NAOTO.
TMP
ANCHOR.

YOU'VE... WORKED VERY HARD.
NOW I SHALL RELEASE YOU.
SNAP

PA-KRAK

ZSH
ZSH
ZSSH
!
BOOM

WHOOSH
WHAT ...?
IT'S OVER?
OH!

RYUZU!
ANCHOR!
OH, THANK GOODNESS. HER INTERNAL PARTS ARE STILL MOVING.
I'LL DO SOME FIRST AID.
NAOTO, YOU WIND UP RYUZU.

WOW, THAT ACTUALLY WORKED, HUH?
NOT THAT I KNOW WHAT HAPPENED IN THAT FIGHT, SINCE IT ONLY LASTED AN INSTANT.

I REALLY COULDN'T BELIEVE THAT SHE ACCEPTED A PLAN THAT INVOLVED USING YOU AS A SHIELD.

I MEAN, NORMALLY, AN AUTOMATON CAN'T DEFY ITS MASTER.
BUT STILL, I CAN'T IMAGINE THAT RYUZU WOULD ACCEPT PUTTING NAOTO IN DANGER...
...EVEN IF IT WAS HER MASTER'S ORDER.

THAT IS ENTIRELY BECAUSE I TRUST MASTER NAOTO.

RYUZU!
MASTER NAOTO EXCEEDS HUMAN STANDARDS IN ALL KINDS OF WAYS.
AND HE HIMSELF SAID THAT HE RELIEVED IN ME.
AND IF MASTER NAOTO SAYS THAT HE TRUSTS ANCHOR, I HAVE NO JUSTIFICATION TO DOUBT HER.
I SEE.
THAT'S SOME RELATIONSHIP YOU HAVE.
I GOTTA SAY, I'M IMPRESSED WITH THE BOTH OF YOU.

I MUST EXTEND MY CURSORY THANKS TO YOU AS WELL, MISS MARIE, FOR ACCOMPANYING US.
TRUST ASIDE, THERE WERE RATIONAL REASONS TO WORRY.
SO WE HAD TO HAVE AN INSURANCE POLICY.

WHOA!
B R R M
AN INCREDIBLE NOISE IS COMING FROM UNDERGROUND.

I DON'T HEAR THE SUPERWEAPON ANYMORE... I GUESS IT'S SETTLED THINGS WITH THE ARMY.
GOOD TO HEAR.
PROVES IT WAS WORTH STARTING THIS WHOLE RUCKUS.

OKAY, THEN LET'S GET ANCHOR BACK TO THE WORKSHOP AND FIX HER.
MEISTER KONRAD'S ARRANGING A SAFE HOUSE FOR US.

I'M SO SLEEPY.
WHERE AM I?
EVERYTHING IN THIS WORLD IS SO STRANGE AND CLOUDY.
EVEN SO...
LOOK, LISTEN!

THAT'S JUST HOW IT IS!
FIRST, IMAGINARY TIME, AND NOW IT'S PERPETUAL MOTION?!
HOW THE HELL DO YOU EXPECT ME TO FIX THAT? ARE YOU PICKING A FIGHT WITH THE UNIVERSE?!
B-DMP
FORGET IT! I'LL FIX HER! GIVE ME THAT SCREW-DRIVER!
AS IF I'D TRUST YOU WITH THIS!
EXPLAIN TO ME JUST HOW YOU PLAN TO DO IT!
RAWR
RAWR
GRAAH!

I'M TELLING YOU, IT'S THE THIRD MANEUVER ON THE RIGHT OF THE 40,325,831ST RESONANCE COUPLING CIRCUIT!
HOW THE HECK DO YOU EVEN GET TO THAT NUMBER? I'M SERIOUSLY GONNA HANG YOU FROM THE CEILING!
WHY IS IT...?
...THIS ALL FEELS SO FAMILIAR.
I MEAN, WHAT IS THIS THING?
THIS FREAKING INCOMPREHENSIBLE, UNIDENTIFIABLE NONSENSE MACHINE!
ALLOW ME TO EXPLAIN IT TO YOU.
FLASH

ANCHOR'S EXCLUSIVE FEATURE IS THE *PERPETUAL GEAR.*
PER IT'S NAME, IT DRIVES HER BODY FROM A SELF-WINDING SPRING WITHOUT USING UP ANY ENERGY. ALL OF THE ENERGY IS CONVERTED TO HEAT, WHICH IS STORED IN HER CUBE.
IT IS THIS INFINITE SUPPLY OF HEAT THAT ALLOWS ANCHOR TO MANIPULATE SPACE, STORE HER ARMAMENTS, AND SUMMON HER EQUIPMENT. IT IS SIMPLE WHEN HER BODY IS CAPABLE OF MOVING PERPETUALLY.
DO YOU UNDER-STAND NOW?
WHAT SHE'S SAYING IS, JUST ROLL WITH IT.
HOW IS THAT POSSIBLE?!
THIS FEELING OF NOS-TALGIA...
...IS JUST LIKE WHEN I WAS FIRST BORN AND EVERYONE WAS HAPPY.

IT MUST BE.
MY HEART REMEMBERS!

BLINK

!
ぱち
BLINK
ぱち
BLINK
GOOD MORNING, ANCHOR!
HOW DO YOU FEEL?

I DON'T KNOW THESE FACES.
I DON'T KNOW THESE VOICES.
WHAT SHOULD I CALL THEM?
IT'S STILL JUST LIKE I REMEMBER, DEEP INSIDE.
I KNOW...
—

DADDY! MOMMY! SISTER!
GOOD MORNING!

CRIK
...
HUH?

DADDY?!
MOMMY?!
AN-CHOR ...
HEY! SHUT UP!
YOU THINK YOU HAVE ANY IDEA HOW I FEEL?
I'M SORRY, IT SEEMS MISS MARIE HAS FAILED TO REPAIR YOU COR-RECTLY.
よよよ... WAVER
SHE JUST CALLED ME THIS FREAK'S WIFE! I HAVE NEVER BEEN SO HUMILIATED!
ANCHORRR, LISTEN CAAARE-FULLY!
BIG BROTHER HERE... HAS BETTER TASTE THAN *THAT*.

OBVIOUSLY, RYUZU IS MY WIFE!
SEE?
I HAVE GOOD TASTE, DON'T I?
I CAN'T CALL YOU...
DADDY?
あ、
んは
GASP
NO, NO, NO! SURE YOU CAN!
I MEAN, IT REALLY STRUCK ME IN MY HEART WHEN YOU SAID THAT!
?
EW.

BUT IF YOU CALL HER MOMMY, IT'LL BE LIKE WE'RE...
たんっ
TUMP
HEY–
?!
WHAT?!
すっ
ぽ
FWUMP
MOMMY!

MARIE! THAT'S NOT FAIR!
SWITCH WITH ME! NOW!
SHUT UP
GET AWAY FROM ME, YOU FREAK!
WHUP
HEY, WHAT IS THIS? DOES SHE REGISTER WHOEVER REPAIRED HER AS HER PARENTS?
NO.
I BELIEVE SHE IS MERELY CONFUSING HER MEMORIES.
LISTEN CARE-FULLY, ANCHOR. YOUR DADDY IS MASTER NAOTO, AND THAT IS ENOUGH.

THIS GIRL IS MERELY SUP-PLEMENTARY.
HEY, WATCH IT.
I CAN'T?
YOU CAN.
IF THAT'S WHAT YOU WANT, YOU CAN CALL HER WHAT-EVER YOU LIKE! YEAH!
LET'S BEAR IT FOR ANCHOR, MOMMY!
GAAAAH!
LEAP

DON'T BE SUCH A CREEP, YOU FREAK!
WHAM!!
GWAAAH?!
SERIOUSLY, THIS IS WRONG! HOW CAN WE FIX THIS?!
AAAAH!
MOMMY...
I TOLD YOU, I'M NOT YOUR...

ACK... SO CUTE...
LURCH
GET IT TO-GETHER, MARIE!
WHY DON'T WE DO THE MASTER AUTHENTI-CATION PROCESS? MAYBE THAT WILL FIX THIS WEIRD IMPRINTING THING.
INDEED.

ANCHOR.
YES, RYUZU?
LET ME CONFIRM: YOU CURRENTLY HAVE NO AUTHORIZED MASTER, CORRECT?
UH-HUH.
VERY WELL.
IN THAT CASE—
す
FUMP
と
っ

THIS IS NAOTO MIURA.
HOW WOULD YOU LIKE TO AUTHORIZE HIM AS YOUR MASTER, AS I HAVE DONE?
DADDY...
...DO YOU WANT TO BE MY MASTER?
WHAT?
YEAH, YEAH!
SURE, I TOTALLY WANNA BE YOUR MASTER!

OKAY.
THEN I'LL START, OKAY?
SST
ス

FWOOSH
?!

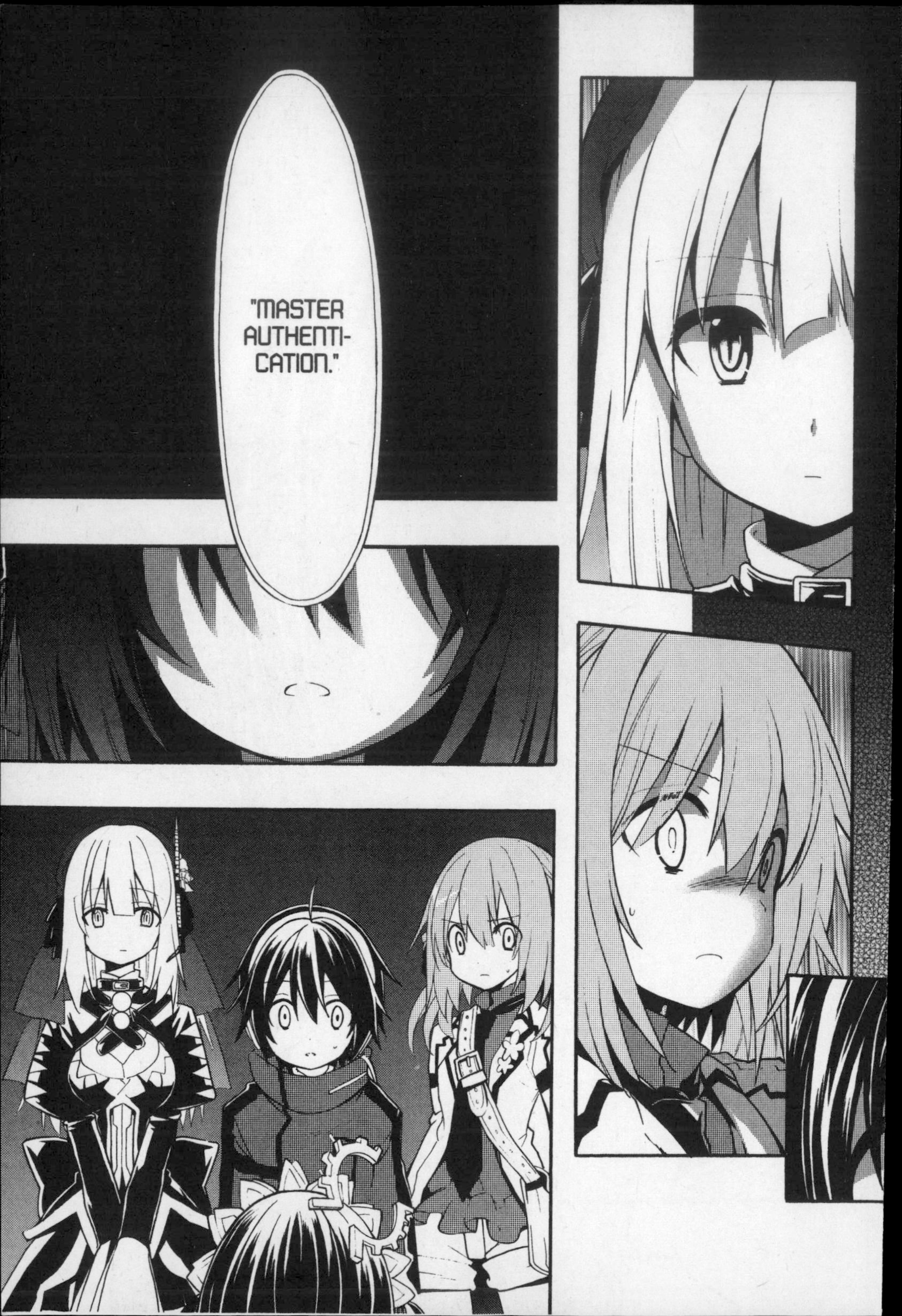

"MASTER AUTHENTI-CATION."

"QUEST-
ION—"
"WHAT
AM I?"

CLOCKWORK
PLANET

Clockwork
Planet

"MASTER AUTHENTICATION."
"QUESTION:
WHAT AM I"
?

Clock 22: Outcry and Resolve

AN-CHOR ...?
YES.
THIS UNIT IS ANCHOR THE TRISHULA.
CORRECT ANSWER TO QUESTION REQUIRED FOR MASTER AUTHENTI-CATION.
AFTER SHE WAS JUST SO FRIENDLY...
UH, SHE'S ACTING SO MECHAN-ICAL ALL OF A SUDDEN.
WHAT'S GOING ON?!

THIS IS ANCHOR'S MASTER AUTHENTI-CATION PROCESS.
IF HE CAN ANSWER HER QUESTION CORRECTLY, HE SHALL BE RECOGNIZED AS HER AUTHORIZED MASTER.
HOW-EVER...
...WHILE IT HARDLY BEARS SAYING, RETRIES ARE NOT PERMITTED.

YOU CAN'T AFFORD TO MESS THIS UP, NAOTO.
BE CAREFUL ...
WHAT ARE YOU? YOU'RE A CUTE LITTLE GIRL.
ISN'T THAT OBVIOUS?
HEY!

HEY!
WOULD YOU LISTEN TO ME?! YOU ONLY GET ONE CHANCE AT THIS!
あ? AND?
BUT I'M RIGHT. THE ANSWER IS RIGHT THERE IN FRONT OF YOU.
ANCHOR'S SUCH A BEAUTIFUL LITTLE GIRL!
はああん AHHHN
OH!
MAYBE THAT SHE'S A LITTLE SISTER?
WHAT MORE DO YOU NEED TO KNOW?
THIS GUY'S BEYOND HOPE...
I GUESS I'M JUST GOING TO HAVE TO COME UP WITH THE RIGHT ANSWER...

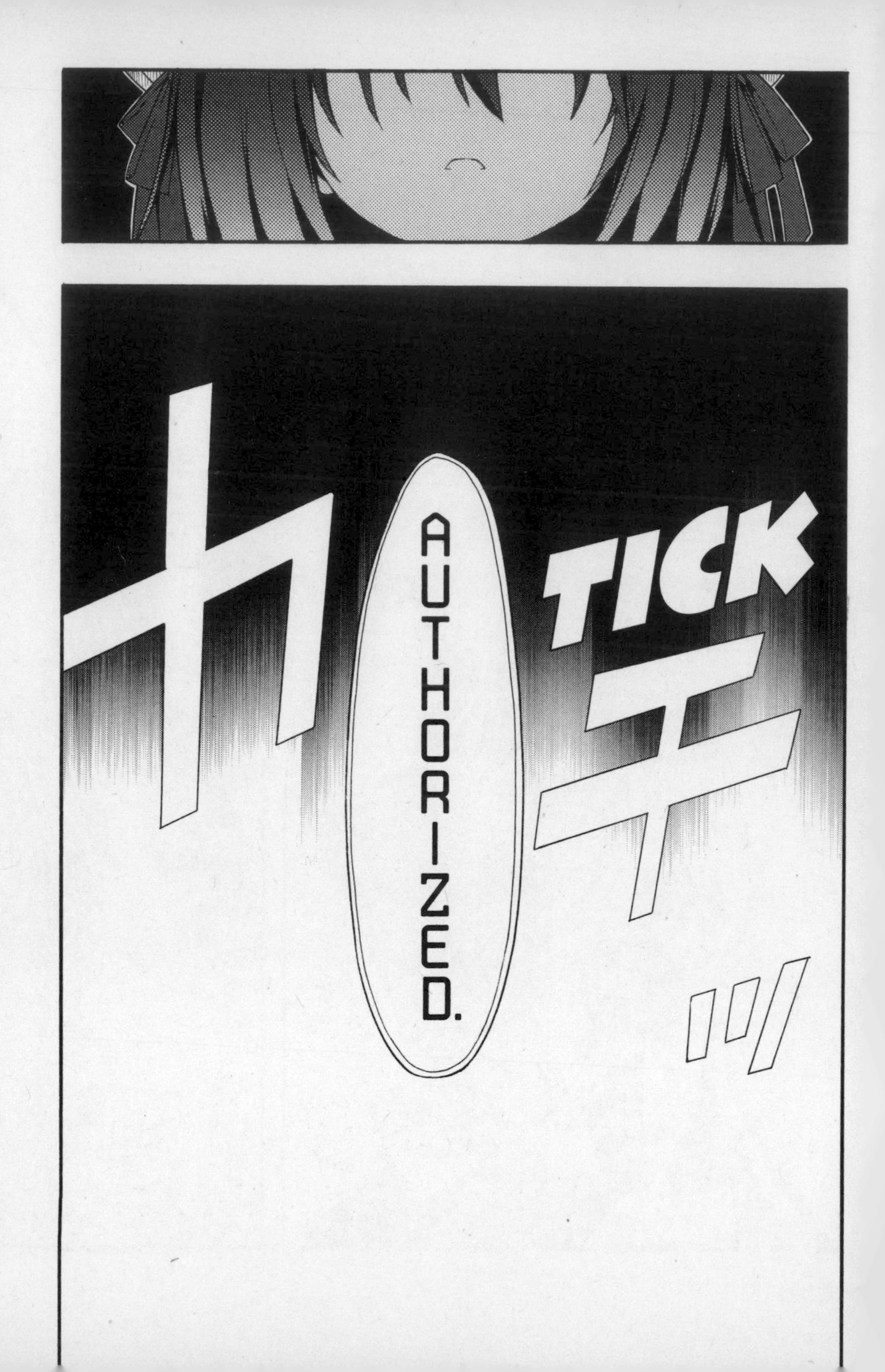
TICK
カチッ
AUTHORIZED.

ALL RIGHT!
WHOOSH!
ONLY MASTER NAOTO COULD PRODUCE THE ANSWER SO QUICKLY.

WONDERFUL SMOOTH SAILING.
HEH HEH!
DUH!
...
HOLD ON A MINUTE. YOU'RE TELLING ME "GIRL" WAS THE RIGHT ANSWER?!
IT WASN'T THE DESIGN CONCEPT, OR SOME MESSAGE FROM Y?
GUESS YOU DON'T GET IT, DO YOU MARIE?
ANCHOR IS A WORK OF ART SO CUTE AND PROVOCATIVE THAT IT MAKES YOU SQUIRM.
SURE, SHE'S GOT A FEW FANCY WEAPONS, BUT THAT'S BESIDE THE POINT.
EH HEH
MASTER NAOTO, YOU ARE BOLD TO CHEAT ON ME WITH MY SISTER.
UH-UM- NO, I MEAN, ANCHOR IS MY DAUGHTER-
...
RUMBLE
YOU LUST FOR YOUR DAUGHTER?
NO, RYUZU! WAIIIT!

INPUT COMMAND.

AN-
CHOR?

YES. UNIT IS ANCHOR THE TRISHULA...
...UNIT IV OF THE INITIAL-Y SERIES.

MASTER IS NAOTO MIURA.
CONFIRMED.

AN-
CHOR.
INPUT COMMAND.

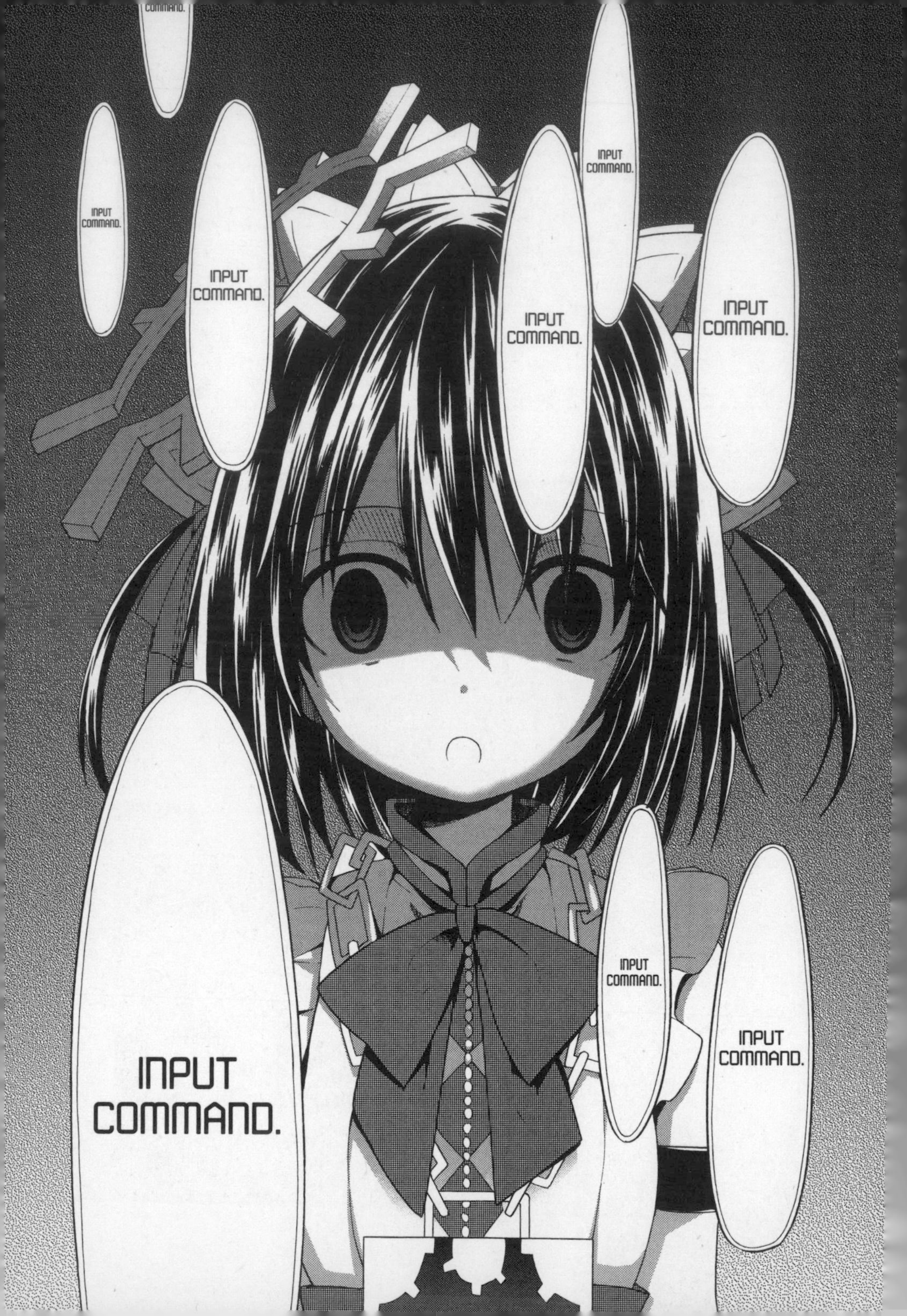

INPUT COMMAND.
INPUT COMMAND.
INPUT COMMAND.
INPUT COMMAND.
INPUT COMMAND.
COMMAND.
INPUT COMMAND.
INPUT COMMAND.
INPUT COMMAND.

WHAT IS THIS?
ARE YOU SURE THAT WAS THE RIGHT ANSWER?
INPUT COM-MAND.
INPUT COM-MAND.
INPUT COM-MAND.
IT WAS, AND ANCHOR IS WORKING PERFECTLY.
YOU CALL THIS WORKING PERFECTLY?!
ANCHOR WAS MANUFACTURED WITH A DESIGN CONCEPT UNIQUE AMONG THE SISTERS.
IT IS THE CONCEPT— OF A WEAPON.

ANCHOR HAS *WILL* IN ORDER TO CONTROL HER POWER WITHOUT A MASTER...
...AND TO HELP HER FIND A SUITABLE MASTER.
HER *WILL* IS A SAFETY MECHANISM.
ONCE SHE FINDS A MASTER, SHE LOSES HER WILL...
...AND FUNCTIONS PURELY AS A WEAPON.

IN OTHER WORDS,
NOW THAT ANCHOR HAS AUTHORIZED A MASTER...
...SHE IS NO LONGER PERMITTED TO HAVE FREE WILL.
...
I DIDN'T SAVE ANCHOR BECAUSE I WANTED A WEAPON.

I SEE.
MASTER NAOTO, I UNDERSTAND THAT YOU CHERISH US.
BUT YOU HAVE NOT FORGOTTEN, HAVE YOU?
THAT WE ARE NOT HUMANS.
WE ARE AUTOMATA.
WE ARE BUT MACHINES WITH UNIQUE FEATURES AND DEFINED CONCEPTS...
...AND ASSIGNED MISSIONS THAT WILL LAST FOREVER.

IT IS OUR PUR-POSE...
...TO FIND A MASTER...
...AND FULFILL THE FUNCTIONS FOR WHICH WE WERE BORN.

THAT BEING SAID...
...MASTER NAOTO, I TRUST THAT YOU ARE CAPABLE OF USING ANCHOR APPROPRIATELY.
USING HER APPROPRIATELY?
WHAT, YOU WANT TO START A WAR?
LOOK, ANCHOR JUST LOST HER WILL AND BECAME A WEAPON!
NO, ANCHOR STILL HAS A WILL.
I KNOW IT.

ANCHOR!
YES. INPUT COM-MAND.
YES.
WHAT DO YOU WANT TO DO, ANCHOR? TELL ME WHAT YOU WANT TO DO.
OBJECTIVE IS TO FUNCTION CORRECTLY AS ANCHOR THE TRISHULA.
THAT'S YOUR *MISSION*, ISN'T IT? ISN'T THERE ANYTHING ELSE YOU WANT TO *DO*?

...
CONFIRMATION: REQUEST DATA DISCLOSURE REGARDING ANCHOR'S FREE WILL?
YES!
FREE WILL LOCKED—
OKAY, THEN HERE'S MY COMMAND.
UNLOCK IT.

...CONFIRMATION: ACTIVATE AUTONOMOUS OPERATION?
UH, YEAH, I GUESS THAT'S WHAT I'M SAYING.

UNDERSTOOD.
CRASH

PERMISSIONS REQUIRED: UNLOCK EMOTION CONTROL CIRCUIT. WAKE UP INDEPENDENT THOUGHT ROUTINE.
AUTHORIZE EXPRESSION OF OPINIONS. PROCEED—
YES, YES!
DO IT ALL!
YOU HAVE MY COMPLETE AND UTTER PERMISSION!
YOU GET IT, ANCHOR?

YOU CAN DO WHAT YOU WANT.
YOU CAN FOLLOW YOUR WILL.

...
I CAN DO...
ANYTHING?

!
OF COURSE!
THEN... GIVE ME...
PERMISSION...
HUH?

GIVE ME...
...PERMISSION...
...TO CRY.

SURE.
YOU CAN CRY.
SURE.
GIVE ME... MORE.
SURE.
CAN I... TOUCH YOU?
SURE.
FFP
とっ
ぴとっ
TUP
CAN I...
...SAY I'M SORRY?
I DON'T THINK YOU HAVE ANYTHING TO APOLOGIZE FOR...
...BUT IF YOU WANT.
ぎゅっ
SQUEEZE

…SORRY.
ぽ
FWUMP
す
I'M SORRY.
I'M SORRY.

ぽろ DRIP
I'M SORRY.
I'M SORRY.
DRIP ぽろ
DRIP ぽろ
I'M SORRY—

CAN I ASK YOU SOME-THING?
DID YOU KNOW THINGS WOULD TURN OUT THIS WAY?
I DID.
HE TRUSTED MASTER NAOTO...
ONE WHO HOLDS THE POWER OF INFINITE VIOLENCE...
...MUST HAVE THE WILL NOT TO EXERCISE IT.
THAT IS Y'S MESSAGE.

I SEE.
CAN I ASK ONE MORE THING?
ON WHAT BASIS DID YOU AUTHORIZE NAOTO AS YOUR MASTER?
THE REASON IS SIMPLE.
...TO *USE ANCHOR* APPROPRIATELY.

OF ALL THE PATHETIC HUMANS DRIFTING ACROSS THE EARTH...
...MASTER NAOTO IS THE FINEST.
AND IN ADDI-TION...

CAN I NOT BREAK ANYTHING ANYMORE?
CAN I NOT KILL ANY-ONE?
SURE!
THERE'S NO NEED FOR ANY OF THAT!

I'M SO GLAD.

ぽ PAT
ん
I WAS CON-VINCED...
...THAT WHERE MASTER NAOTO IS GOING... IS WHERE I WILL FOLLOW.
I GUESS I WAS THE ONLY ONE WORRIED.
WELL, HEY. ONE MORE THING SETTLED.
FWOOP

WHIRL
WHOA!
THIS SPATIAL DISTORTION...
...OPENS THE WAY TO ANCHOR'S ARMORY.
CRACK
ZLIP
CRACK
THUD
AAH!
SOMETHING CAME OUT!

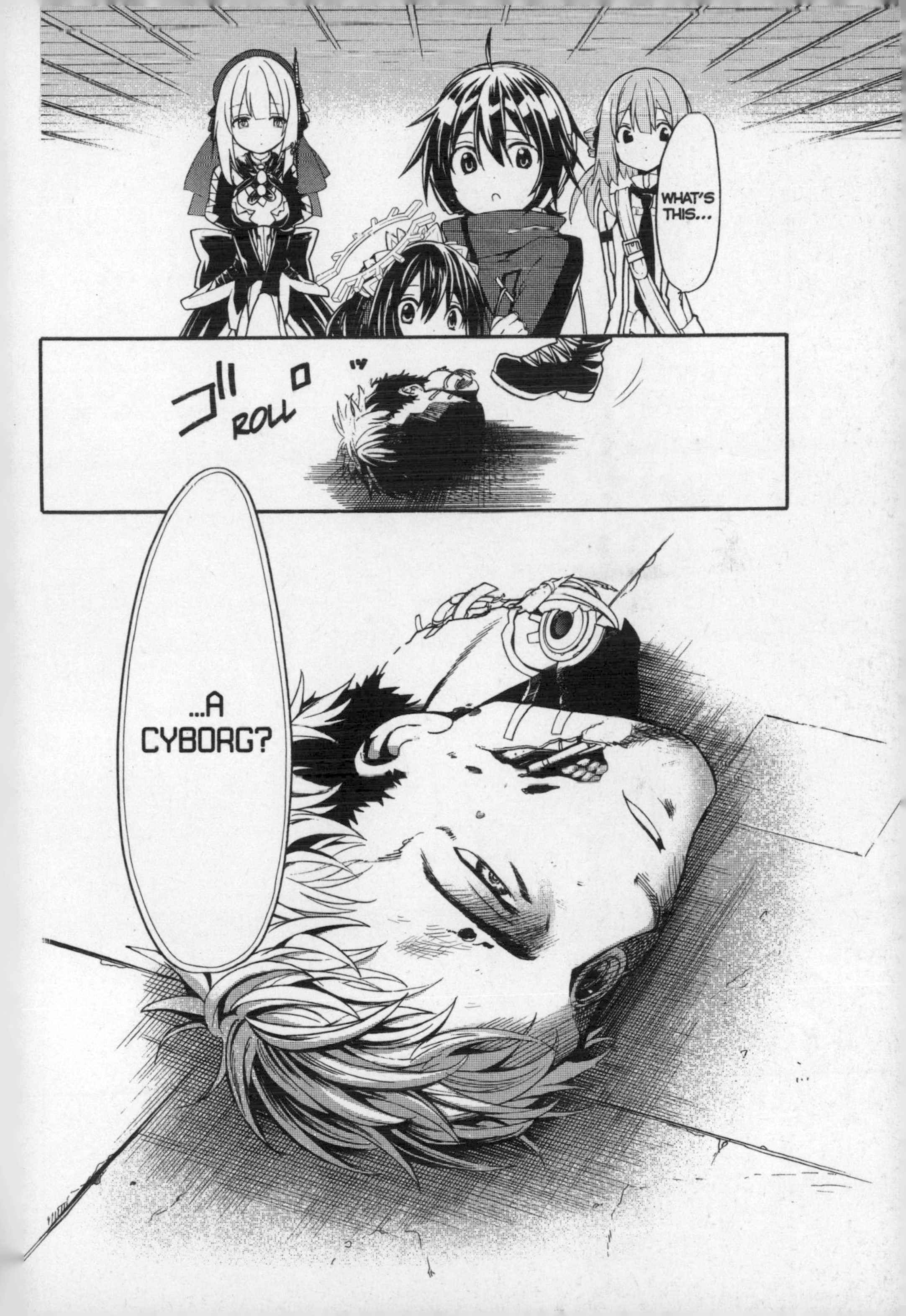
WHAT'S THIS...
ゴロッ
ROLL
...A CYBORG?

CLOCKWORK
PLANET

Clockwork Planet

A CYBORG?
ゴロン
ROLL

WHAT'S SOME GUY'S HEAD DOING HERE?
IS HE DEAD?
POKE
WOW
I DON'T KNOW. LET'S FIX HIM AND SEE.
I CAN PROBABLY GET HIM TALKING AGAIN AT LEAST.
DOESN'T LOOK LIKE YOUR AVERAGE COMMERCIAL MODEL.
I'M GUESSING THIS IS CUSTOM EQUIPMENT USING SECRET TECH, MAYBE?
BUT SEEING HOW BEAT-UP HE LOOKS...

...HE PROBABLY FOUGHT WITH ANCHOR WHEN SHE HAD THE MASK ON...
...AND GOT WARPED OUT OF SIGHT, WHERE HE'S BEEN EVER SINCE.
STATIC
OH!
HE WORKS NOW!
TWITCH
GH-
FLARE
TWITCH

HEY.
YOU AWAKE?
WHAT?
WHAT'S –
UH.
YOU'RE ...
MARIE BELL BRE-GUET?
NOD
AREN'T YOU CLEVER.
...
HFF.
SO, WHAT, AM I IN HELL?
GRIN

YOU'RE NOT DEAD. I'M ALIVE, TOO.
IN OTHER WORDS, HELL.
THIS IS REALITY.
I'M VERMOUTH. NICE TO MEET YOU, KID.
BY THE WAY, COULD I BUM A SMOKE?

Clock 24: Weapon and Human

HMM...
FEB-RUARY 8TH IN TOKYO?
I HAVE NO IDEA HOW I'M STILL ALIVE...
...BUT THINGS MUST'VE WORKED OUT BETTER THAN EXPECTED, HUH?
WHAT DO YOU MEAN?
WELL, IF YOU'RE HERE, THAT MEANS THE MESSAGE MADE ITS WAY TO THE GHOST, RIGHT?
TWITCH
MESSAGE...
—HEY, WENCH.

RUMBLE
SEEMS LIKE YOU'RE GETTING AROUND A LOT FOR A GHOST GIRL. IS YOUR HOLE SUFFERING FROM A LACK OF ATTENTION?
THERE ARE FOLKS WAITING TO SCREW YOU WITH THEIR LITTLE BIG COCKS ANYTIME YOU'RE READY, YOU KNOW?
RUMBLE
WHY DON'T YOU COME SHAKE YOUR CUTE BUTT OVER HERE AND BEG, YA NYMPHO.
OH, I SEE. SO IT WAS YOU.
YOU'RE THE FOOL WITH NO REGARD FOR HIS OWN LIFE WHO SENT A MESSAGE TALKING TRASH ABOUT MARIE BELL BREGUET.
RUMBLE
EXACTLY.
SURE IS REASSURING TO SEE THAT YOU DO EXACTLY WHAT WE PROVOKED YOU TO DO.
CHATTER
CHATTER
YOU SURE LIVE UP TO YOUR REPUTATION AS A PSYCHO.
BUT I NEVER GUESSED JUST HOW FRUSTRATED YOU WERE–
HEH
I'M GETTIN' OLD, YA KNOW? IF YOU WANT ME TO PAY ATTENTION TO YA, YOU'D BETTER SHAKE YOUR BUTT AND BE–

ZHONK
SO, MONGREL...
RUMBLE
FLINCH
...YOU'D BETTER BE CAREFUL NOT TO GET TOO CHEEKY WITH ME, OR I'LL CUT OFF YOUR HEAD AND SHOVE IT DOWN THE TOILET. ♥
GRIND
GRIND
GRIND

YOU'RE BEING A BAD INFLUENCE ON ANCHOR COULD YOU TAKE THIS ELSEWHERE?
FWOOM
YOU THINK I'M ANY KIND OF INFLUENCE ON AN AUTOMATON WHO'S BEEN IN OPERATION FOR 1,000 YEARS?
!
AREN'T YOUR PANTIES A BIT TOO CHILDISH?
IF YOU'RE NOT GONNA WEAR SEXIER ONES, YOU MIGHT AS WELL JUST TAKE THOSE OFF.
YOU REALLY WANT ME TO MURDER YOU, DON'T YOU?!
HEY THERE, PRIN-CESS.
TAKE THIS!
AND THIS!
BAM
BAM

WHAT'S ALL THE FUSS ABOUT?
!
YOU!

AREN'T YOU VAINNEY HALTER?
HUH?
GLINT

HEY, MARIE, WHO'S THIS HALF-DEAD LITTLE PUNK?
AW, YOU DON'T GOTTA BE LIKE THAT. I'M YOUR BIGGEST FAN.

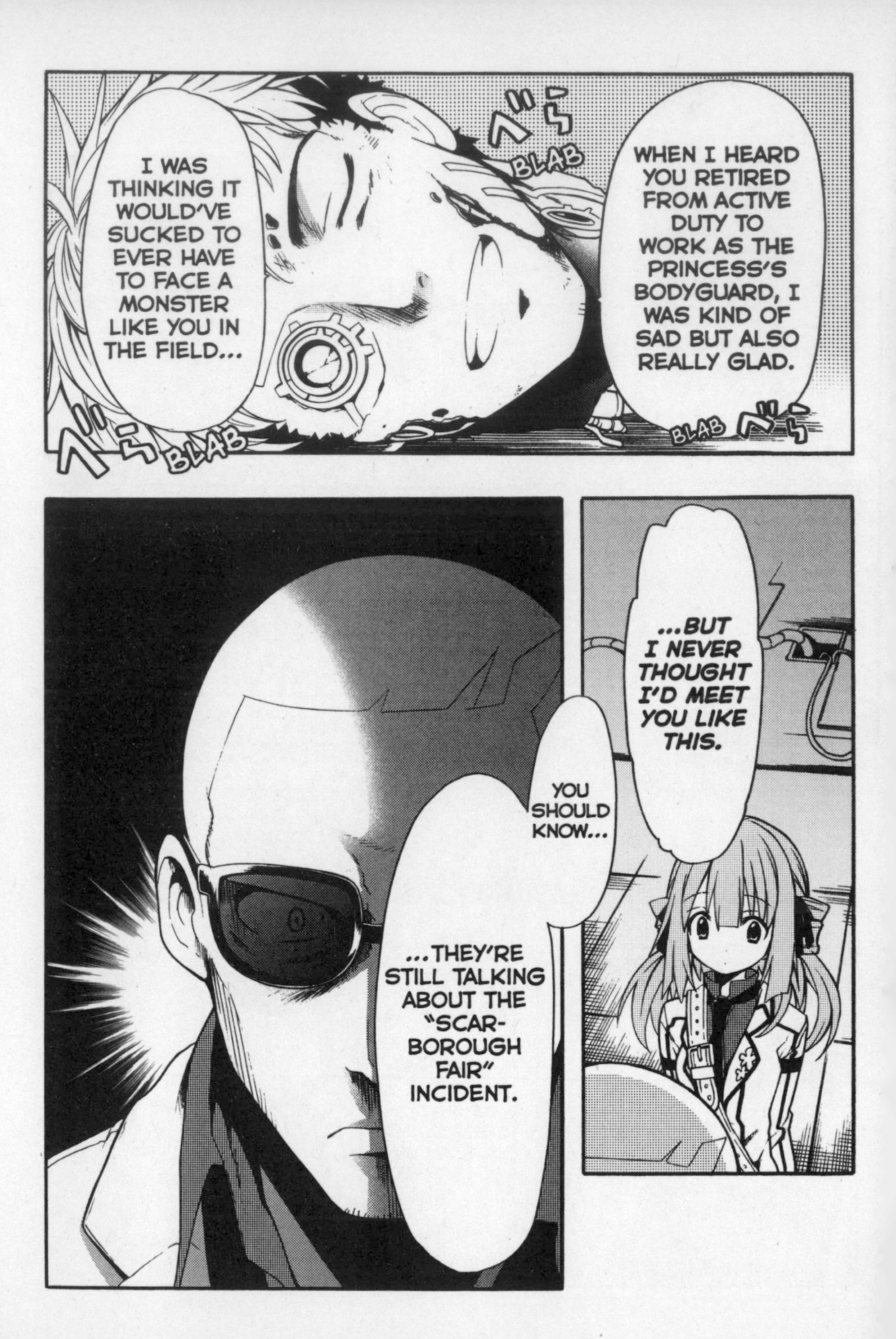
BLAB
WHEN I HEARD YOU RETIRED FROM ACTIVE DUTY TO WORK AS THE PRINCESS'S BODYGUARD, I WAS KIND OF SAD BUT ALSO REALLY GLAD.
BLAB
I WAS THINKING IT WOULD'VE SUCKED TO EVER HAVE TO FACE A MONSTER LIKE YOU IN THE FIELD...
BLAB
...BUT I NEVER THOUGHT I'D MEET YOU LIKE THIS.
YOU SHOULD KNOW...
...THEY'RE STILL TALKING ABOUT THE "SCAR-BOROUGH FAIR" INCIDENT.

LOOK, JUST WHO ARE YOU?
SWAY...
WHERE DID YOU COME FROM, AND WHAT ARE YOU HERE FOR?
...
HOW IS IT POSSIBLE YOU'RE STILL ALIVE?
GLARE
UH...
WOULD THAT BE...
...BECAUSE ANCHOR IS DESIGNED NOT TO KILL HUMANS?
HEY, NOW.
MY TEAM GOT WIPED OUT BY THAT THING.
ARE YOU SAYING CYBORGS AREN'T HUMAN?
GLANCE
HMM.
THAT'S INTER-ESTING.

SHE ATTACKED ME WHEN WE FIRST MET.
AND SHE DID IN ALL OF THIS PUNK'S FRIENDS, BUT LEFT HIM ALIVE ...
WHAT KINDA CRI-TERIA IS SHE USING ?
PRO-BABLY ...
...HUMAN-NESS?
HUH?

YEAH, REMEMBER?
YOU WERE GONNA ABANDON RYUZU AND ME.
YOU WEREN'T EVEN THINKING ABOUT YOUR OWN LIFE...
WHOOSH
...ALL YOU WERE THINKING ABOUT WAS GETTING MARIE OUT OF THERE, RIGHT?

I SEE.
SO YOU MEAN ANCHOR DIDN'T RECOGNIZE HALTER AS HUMAN.
HUMAN...
VERMOUTH... THIS GUY SENT ME A MESSAGE WHEN HE WAS ABOUT TO DIE...
I GUESS IN HIS LAST MOMENTS, HE RE-TURNED TO BEING HUMAN AFTER BEING A MACHINE.
AW,
DON'T LOOK SO SERIOUS, POPS.
IT'S NOT LIKE THIS SEVERED HEAD IS GONNA SELF-DESTRUCT ON US. CHILL OUT.

...
OH— HEY!
IT'S NOT LIKE I'M BLAMING YOU.
I GET IT. IT'S YOUR JOB!
I MEAN, JEEZ, YOU'RE LIKE, SO RESOLUTE AND STUFF!
OH, YOU!
YOU'RE SO-COOL!
... YEAH.
I GOTTA SAY, IT MAKES ME THINK.

AN AUTOMATON EVALUATED MY HUMANITY AND FOUND ME LACKING?
?
DAMN, THAT STINGS.
STREGA... AMARETTO...
MURMUR
I NEVER EVEN LEARNED THEIR REAL NAMES.
HUH?
YOU SAY SOMETHING?
NAH, IT'S NOTHING.
OH.
HM.

ALL RIGHT.
SO WE'VE CLEANED UP ALL THE EVIDENCE OF OUR LITTLE PLOT, RIGHT?
YEAH.
MEISTER KONRAD AND HIS GUYS ARE GONE ALREADY.
EVERY-ONE'S ALIBIS LOOK AIR-TIGHT.
PLUNK
EXCEPT FOR NAOTO, THAT IS.
TRUE THAT.
AREN'T YOU GLAD, NAOTO? YOUR NAME'LL BE IN THE TEXTBOOKS!
IS ANYONE GONNA BELIEVE I PULLED OFF A TERROR ATTACK THIS BIG BY MYSELF?

SHE MEANS THAT YOU HAVE AT LEAST COME TO EARN GLOBAL RECOGNITION, MASTER NAOTO.
EH HEH HEH...
NAH, IT'S NOT LIKE...
AS A ONCE-IN-A-CENTURY EPIC VILLAIN, BUT STILL.
DADDY, YOU'RE AMAZING!
HUG
OH CRAP, THIS BLISS I'M FEELING RIGHT NOW COULD PROBABLY LEAD ME TO ATTAIN ENLIGHTEN-MENT.
EH HEH HEH HEH
DAZED
STOP MESSING AROUND. LET'S GET OUT OF HERE.

YOU KNOW, PRINCESS, DO WE REALLY NEED TO KEEP THIS PIECE OF TRASH?
HEY, NO NEED TO CALL ME TRASH, ALL RIGHT? YOU GIVE ME A NEW BODY, AND I'LL BE BACK TO NORMAL. I'LL WORK FOR YOU AND RETURN THE FAVOR.

HEH. WHAT WE'RE GONNA DO IS EXPLOIT THE CRAP OUT OF YOU. GET READY.

A NUMBER OF THINGS HAVE HAPPENED IN THE LAST FEW DAYS.
WE FOUND A MASSIVE WEAPON HIDDEN UNDERGROUND, LEARNED OF A MILITARY CONSPIRACY, AND LAUNCHED A TERROR ATTACK ON AKIHABARA.
THESE TWO FACED A SITUATION THAT MOST WOULD DISMISS AS A LOST CAUSE...
...AND BROKE THROUGH.
PERHAPS IT IS TRUE...

...THEY WORK ALONG DIFFERENT LINES...
...YET THEIR POTENTIAL...
WHAT'S
THAT SOUND?

WHOOM
WHAT?!
WHAT JUST HAPPEN-ED?

NO WAY...
IT'S THAT THING...

THAT SUPER-WEAPON ...
CRASH
...IT'S SMASHING ITS WAY UP THROUGH THE GROUND!
CRASH
IS THIS A JOKE?
WHAT ARE THE TOKYO ARMED FORCES DOING?!
DIDN'T THEY FINISH IT?!
HEY, GIRLY, YOU PUT THE ARMY UP AGAINST THAT THING?!
I HAD NO OTHER OPTION !!!

WHY DO YOU THINK I BOTHERED TO USE RADIO?
THEY WERE DOING RESEARCH AGAINST INTER-NATIONAL AGREE-MENTS IN SHIGA.
RESEARCH-ING THE SAME THING THAT LED TO THE PURGE: ELECTRO-MAGNETIC TECH-NOLOGY.
THAT MONSTER IS WHAT ALL THAT RESEARCH WAS BUILDING UP TO. DON'T YOU GET IT?

ゴゴ
RUMBLE
ゴ
RUMBLE
WHY ...
...DIDN'T I THINK OF THAT?
ゴ
ゴ
RUMBLE
ゴ
RUMBLE
CLOCKWORK PLANET'S GREATEST WEAKNESS...
IS THAT THERE IS ONE THING CAPABLE OF DISTURBING THE FUNC- TION OF ALL THE GEARS.
ゴ
NAMELY ...
YOU'RE SAYING THAT WEAPON ...

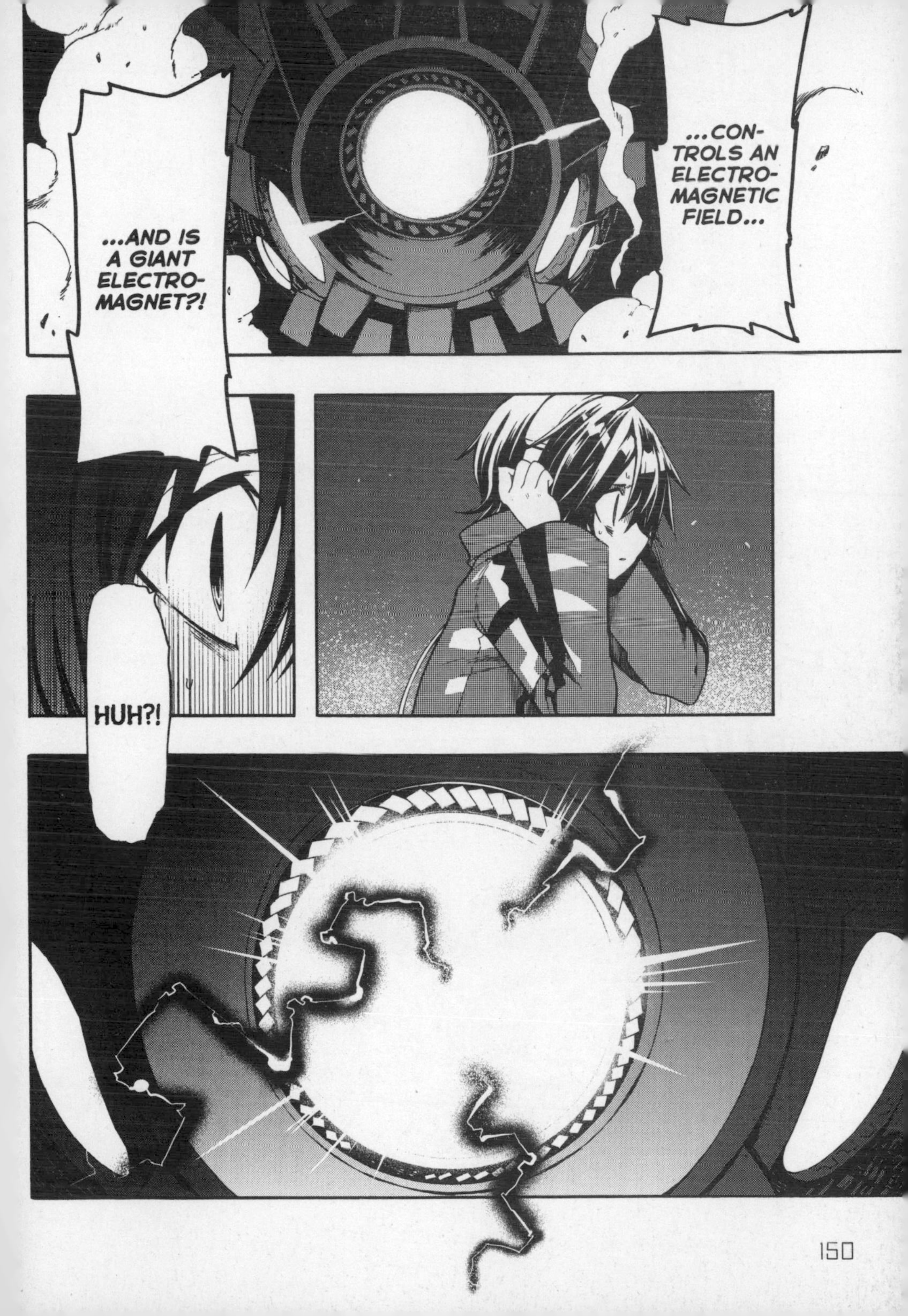

...CON-
TROLS AN
ELECTRO-
MAGNETIC
FIELD...
...AND IS
A GIANT
ELECTRO-
MAGNET?!
HUH?!

ZZZT
ZZZT

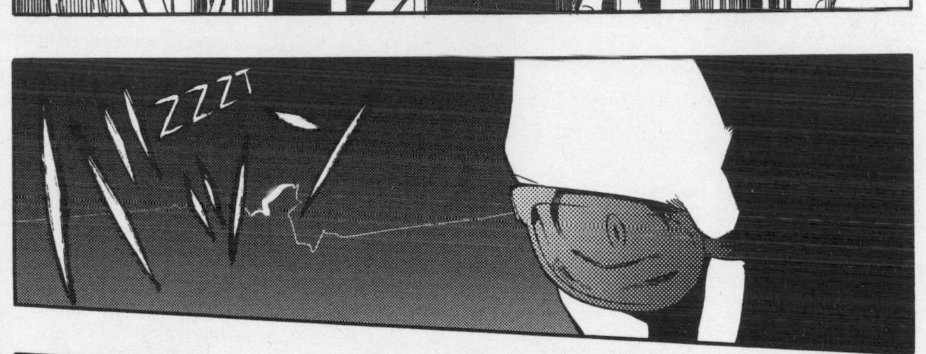
ZZZZT

HI
HH...
WHUMP

WHUMP

FLICKER
FLIT
FLIT
ZZT

ARRIVED ON SURFACE. NO THREAT FOUND. PROCEEDING WITH SEARCH FOR THE ENEMY.
MAIN CANNON COOLING 14 PERCENT. ENERGY RECHARGE 3 PERCENT.
RECAL-CULATING TIME UNTIL RE-CHARGED.
CAN I JUST LET IT END LIKE THIS AFTER SEEING THAT?
GRIND
THAT BOY I MET UNDER-GROUND...

WE HAVEN'T LOST HOPE!
... THOSE EYES...
...SO FREE OF DOUBT...
... CHANGED "POSSI-BILITY" ...
...INTO "CONVIC-TION" FOR ME.
HE IS THE MASTERMIND BEHIND CLOCKWORK PLANET.
YES.

THAT BOY...
...IS Y.

Clockwork
Planet

Clockwork
Planet

GRID AKIHABARA AIRSPACE
UNKNOWN MASSIVE WEAPON IN GRID AKIHABARA.
DESTROY IT.
ROAR
TCH.

*Airborne Warning and Control System.

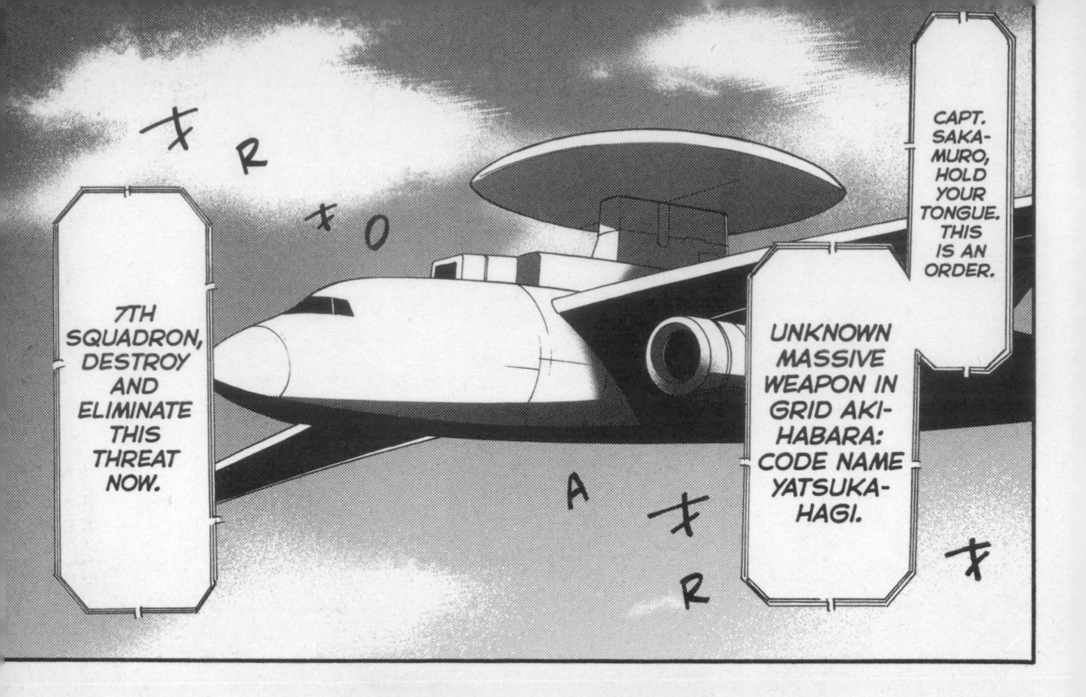
CAPT. SAKAMURO, HOLD YOUR TONGUE. THIS IS AN ORDER.
UNKNOWN MASSIVE WEAPON IN GRID AKIHABARA: CODE NAME YATSUKAHAGI.
7TH SQUADRON, DESTROY AND ELIMINATE THIS THREAT NOW.
ROAR

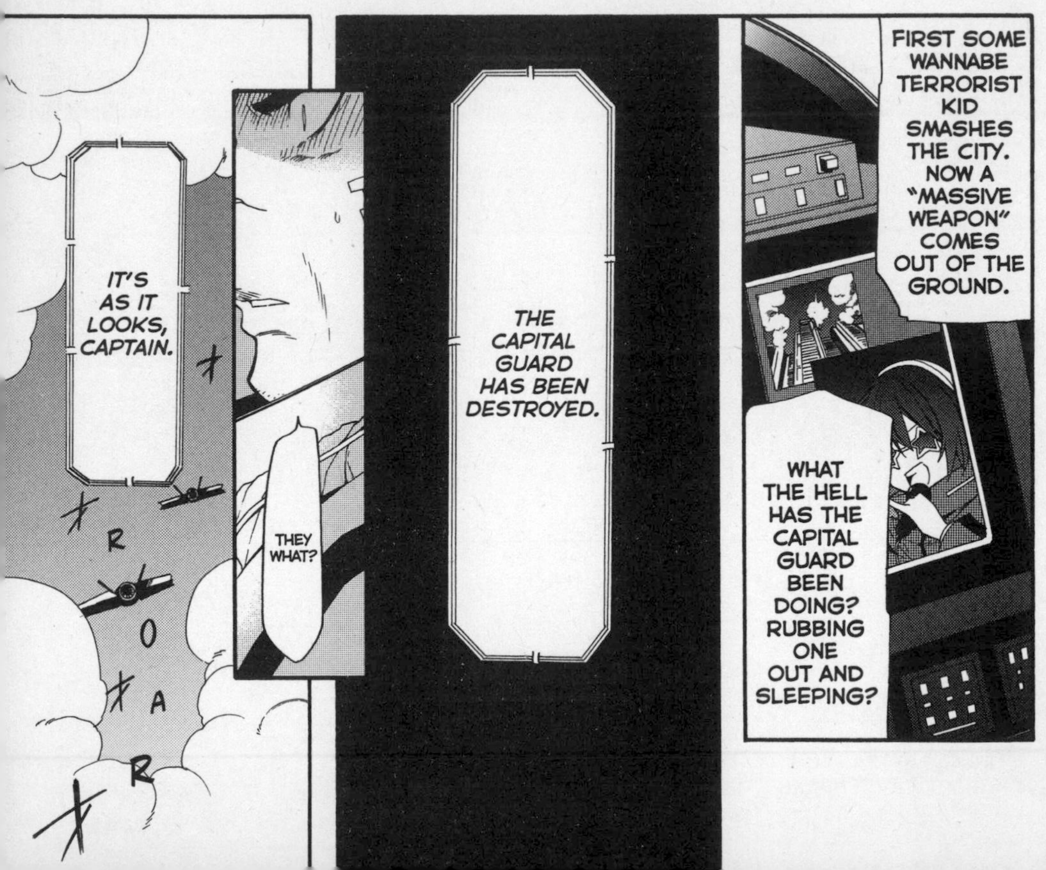
FIRST SOME WANNABE TERRORIST KID SMASHES THE CITY. NOW A "MASSIVE WEAPON" COMES OUT OF THE GROUND.
WHAT THE HELL HAS THE CAPITAL GUARD BEEN DOING? RUBBING ONE OUT AND SLEEPING?
THE CAPITAL GUARD HAS BEEN DESTROYED.
THEY WHAT?
IT'S AS IT LOOKS, CAPTAIN.
ROAR

THE THREAT IS REAL.
IF GRID AKIHABARA GOES DOWN...
Clock 25: Yatsukahagi

...TOKYO—
NO, EVEN
JAPAN—
WILL GO
WITH IT.
PROVE
YOUR-
SELVES,
SOLDIERS!

THE CAPITAL GUARD WAS THE MOST POWERFUL UNIT IN ALL OF THE ARMED FORCES OF JAPAN.
AND NOW IT'S GONE...
AND THE POLITICIANS DIDN'T KNOW WHAT TO DO BUT SCREAM FOR THE AIR FORCE TO COVER THEIR BACKS...
DAMN THEM!

CLOSING.
HEADS UP, EVERY-ONE!

THE BRASS TELLS US... THE NATURE, NUMBER, AND RANGE OF THE TARGET'S WEAPONS ARE UNKNOWN.
ROGER THAT.

STORM ONE TO ALL UNITS: FORMATION DELTA.
IT'S A BURST-AND-RUN.
GRIN
FIRE ALL BULLETS FROM MAXIMUM RANGE AND GET THE HELL OUT!
WHAT?
CAPTAIN!
THOSE ARE NOT YOUR ORDERS! DEFER TO THE TACTI-CAL—
TACTI-CAL? YOUR ORDERS ARE "SMASH THAT DAMN YATSU-KAHAGI" AND YOU CALL THAT TACTI-CAL?
ROAR
HOW TO SMASH IT IS MY GOD-DAMN JOB!

I'LL CARRY OUT THE ORDER. THAT'S MY DUTY AS A SOLDIER.
BUT I ALSO HAVE A DUTY TO NOT THROW AWAY MY MEN'S LIVES FOR NOTHING.
YOU GOT IT, GUYS? DON'T DIE.
I'LL TAKE RESPON-SIBILITY.
ROAR
WILCO!
SAKA-MURO!
YOU SON OF A-! AFTER THIS MISSION-

BOOM
–I'LL SEE YOU IN COURT–
BZZZT

WH- WHAT WAS THAT?!
WE'RE DISCONNECTED?!
HEY, DON'T KID WITH ME!
DON'T TELL ME... THAT MONSTER TOOK DOWN THE AWACS?!
IF IT CAN SHOOT DOWN THE AWACS 20,000 METERS ABOVE US—
—THAT MEANS WE'RE ALL WELL WITHIN ITS RANGE ALREADY!
IT'S TAUNTING US!

ALL UNITS! EVADE! SPREAD OUT! TURN! USE YOUR AFTER-BURNERS!
BUG OUT— WE'RE IN RANGE!
W– WILCO!
ROAR

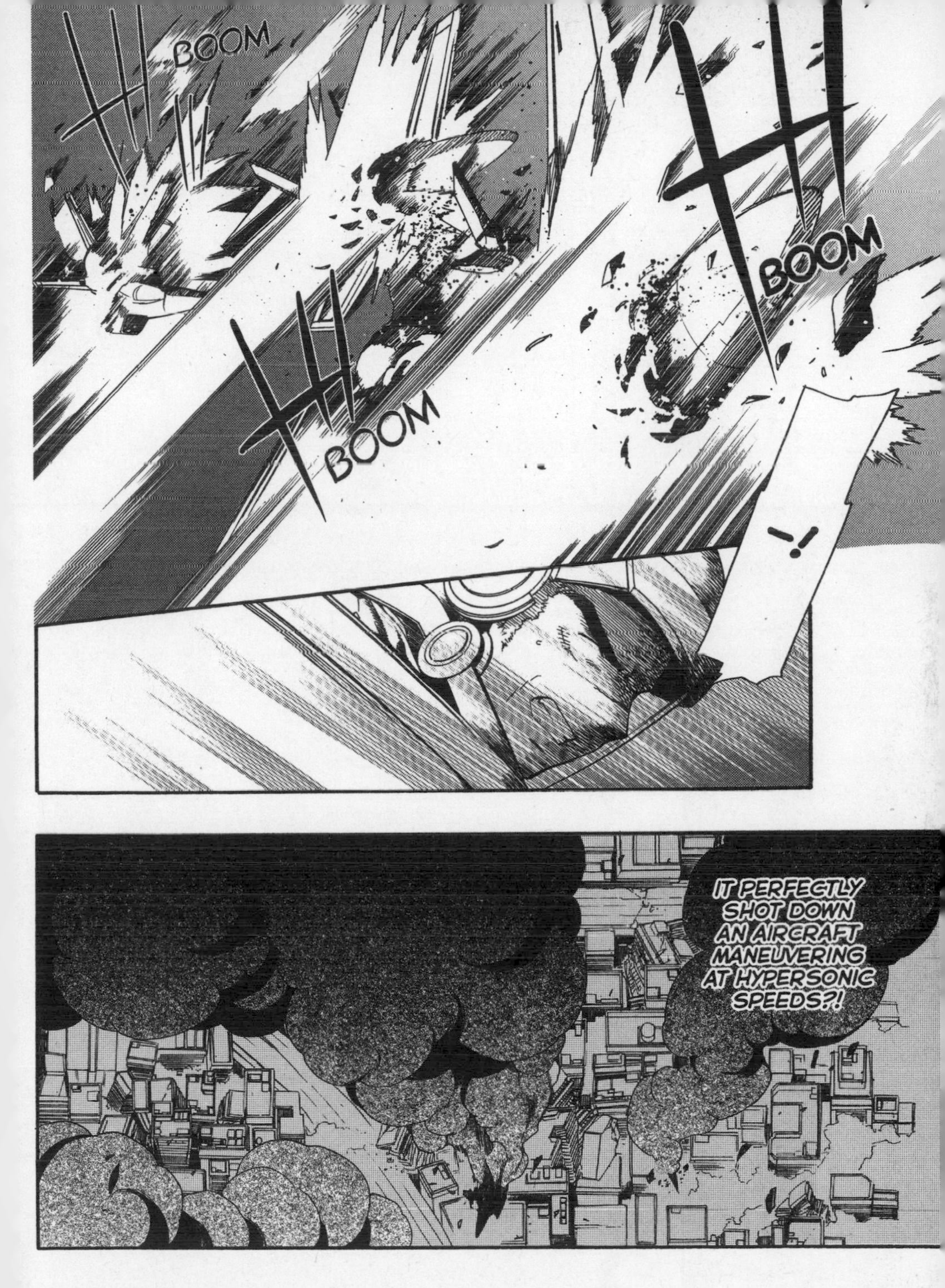
BOOM
BOOM
BOOM
--!
IT PERFECTLY SHOT DOWN AN AIRCRAFT MANEUVERING AT HYPERSONIC SPEEDS?!

IT'S COMING!
DAMN IT!
GRNK
VOOM
ROAR
CRACK
CRACK

BOOOM
I ESCAPED AN ATTACK BY A HAIR'S BREADTH...
THE HELL!
I'M FLYING AT FIVE TIMES THE SPEED OF SOUND! WHY CAN'T I SEE ANYTHING?

IT'S NOT A LASER. IT'S NOT A RESONANCE CANNON.
IT'S TOO FAST AND PRECISE TO BELIEVE–
–IT'S A BULLET OF MAGIC.
–
STORM ONE TO ALL UNITS! ABANDON YOUR AIRCRAFT! BAIL OUT–
–NOW!
WILCO!
SHUNK

WHOOSH
"YATSUKAHAGI." AN UNKNOWN MASSIVE WEAPON—YOU COULD JUST CALL IT OUR TARGET. WHY BOTHER WITH A CODE NAME?
THEY KNOW...
AT THE VERY LEAST, THE BRASS KNOWS WHAT IT'S HERE FOR.
GRIND

GOD-
DAMN
POLITI-
CIANS!
WHAT
IN THE
WORLD
ARE YOU
MESSING
WITH?!

!
ROAR
KABOOOM

SO WHEN THE CAPITAL GUARD AND THE AIR FORCE BOTH FAIL...
...THEY DECIDE TO USE THE CAPITAL DEFENSE CANNON...

FWOOM
DAMN... YOU CALL THAT A "TRUMP CARD"? DIDN'T EVEN SCRATCH THE GUY.
RUMBLE
WHO'S GONNA PAY FOR ALL THIS DAMAGE?

GRID KASUMIGASEKI
CONFERENCE OF THE RULING PARTY
THE SITUATION COULD NOT BE WORSE.
FIRST, THE LATE-NIGHT TERROR IN GRID AKIHABARA ROBBED US OF CONTROL OF THE CITY FUNCTIONS...
...AND NOW, AN ARMED FACTION HAS OCCUPIED AKIHABARA WITH AN UNKNOWN MASSIVE WEAPON.

WE MUST DESTROY THIS WEAPON IMMEDIATELY.
IT'S ONLY A MATTER OF TIME BEFORE IT AFFECTS THE OTHER GRIDS.
WELL, YOU SEE...
IT WIPED OUT BOTH THE CAPITAL GUARD AND THE 7TH SQUADRON.
THOSE WERE THE TWO GREATEST FORCES THE STATE HAD!
BAM
HOW COULD THEY FAIL TO SUPPRESS A TERROR ATTACK BY SOME KID?!
WHAT IS THIS LAND'S DEFENSE COMIN' TO?!
WHSH
THE ROLE OF THE MINISTRY OF DEFENSE IS TO PROTECT THE COUNTRY FROM FOREIGN INVASIONS.
THE SCENARIO OF A WEAPON OF MASS DESTRUCTION EMERGING FROM OUR OWN SOIL WAS NOT ANTICIPATED.
THEN JUST WHAT DO YOU PROPOSE WE DO?!
RIGHT...

THE CAPITAL DEFENSE CANNON:
A MASSIVE BATTERY OF EXTREME RANGE POSITIONED ATOP MOUNT FUJI.
JAPAN'S TRUMP CARD IN THE CASE OF INVASION OF THE CAPITAL BY A FOREIGN POWER.
IF NEITHER THE CAPITAL GUARD NOR THE AIR FORCE IS CAPABLE OF FIGHTING IT...
...YOU COULD USE THE CAPITAL DEFENSE CANNON–
SIR...
...IT HAS BEEN USED.
BUT...

...THE TARGET'S ARMOR...
...SEEMS TO HAVE RESISTED ALL SIGNIFICANT DAMAGE.
THE CAPITAL DEFENSE CANNON...
DOESN'T WORK?
DAMN IT ALL! IT'S ALL OVER!
SHUDDER
GWISH
GWISH
WHO CAN WE TURN TO NOW?
AT THIS RATE, TOKYO... NO, JAPAN WILL SINK!

WITHIN THE YATSUKAHAGI
WHAT REMARKABLE RESULTS, YOUR EXCELLENCY.
TO ELIMINATE THE CAPITAL GUARD AND THE 7TH SQUADRON WITH SUCH EASE!
AND EVEN TO WITHSTAND DIRECT BOMBARDMENT FROM THE CAPITAL DEFENSE CANNON, THOUGHT TO BE JAPAN'S TRUMP CARD AGAINST BOTH GROUND AND AIR ATTACKS!

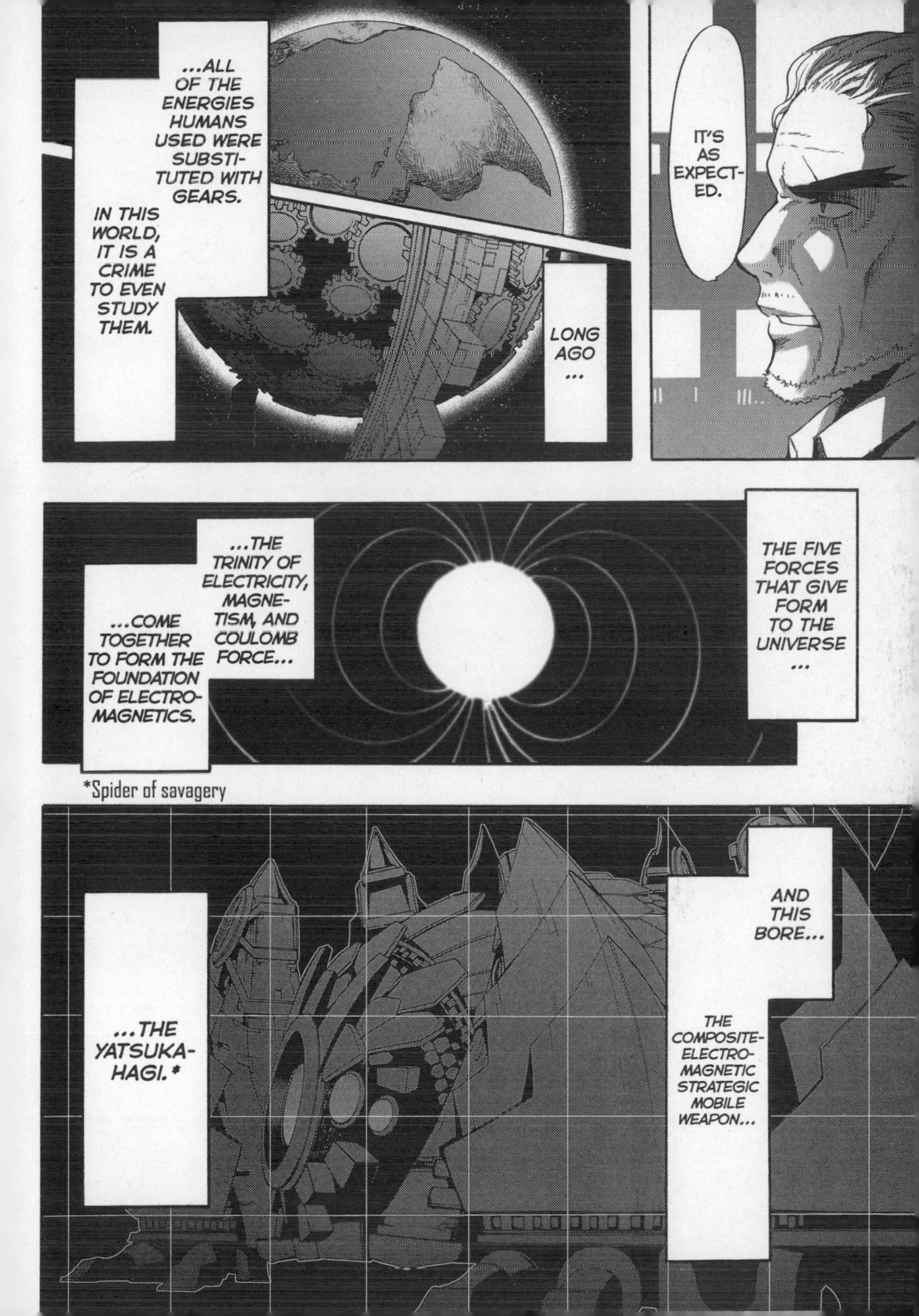

IT'S AS EXPECTED.
LONG AGO...
...ALL OF THE ENERGIES HUMANS USED WERE SUBSTITUTED WITH GEARS.
IN THIS WORLD, IT IS A CRIME TO EVEN STUDY THEM.
THE FIVE FORCES THAT GIVE FORM TO THE UNIVERSE...
...THE TRINITY OF ELECTRICITY, MAGNETISM, AND COULOMB FORCE...
...COME TOGETHER TO FORM THE FOUNDATION OF ELECTROMAGNETICS.
AND THIS BORE...
THE COMPOSITE-ELECTROMAGNETIC STRATEGIC MOBILE WEAPON...
...THE YATSUKAHAGI.*

*Spider of savagery

BEFORE THIS, ANY CLOCKWORK WEAPON IS BUT A TOY.
WHEN FOREIGN POWERS SEE THIS, THEY WILL HAVE NO CHOICE BUT TO ACKNOWLEDGE THE EFFECTIVENESS OF OUR RESEARCH.
THE TOKYO ARMED FORCES...
...HAVE NO ONE LEFT WHO CAN STOP US!
EVEN SO...
...THIS IS OF NO INTEREST TO ME.

WE ONLY PAID THEM BACK WHAT WE OWED.
US AND THE GOVERNMENT, WE ARE THE SAME. IN FACT, WE'VE BEEN DOING THE SAME THINGS OVER AND OVER SINCE ANCIENT TIMES.
HUMAN-KIND CANNOT CHANGE.
AND YET...
GRIND

...HOW DID Y DO IT?

A MERE HUMAN BEING, INCAPABLE OF CHANGE—SOMEHOW Y MANAGED TO CREATE THIS ENORMITY—THIS MONSTROSITY: CLOCKWORK PLANET.
WHO WAS Y?

EVERY-ONE DEVOTED THEIR LIVES TO BECOME LIKE Y.
ONLY ...
TO HAVE THEIR DREAMS CRUSHED.
I'D GIVEN UP HOPE IN THE WORLD. I'D THOUGHT I WAS DONE WITH THIS LIFE.
CREAK...
T . .

UNTIL I LAID EYES ON THAT BOY—

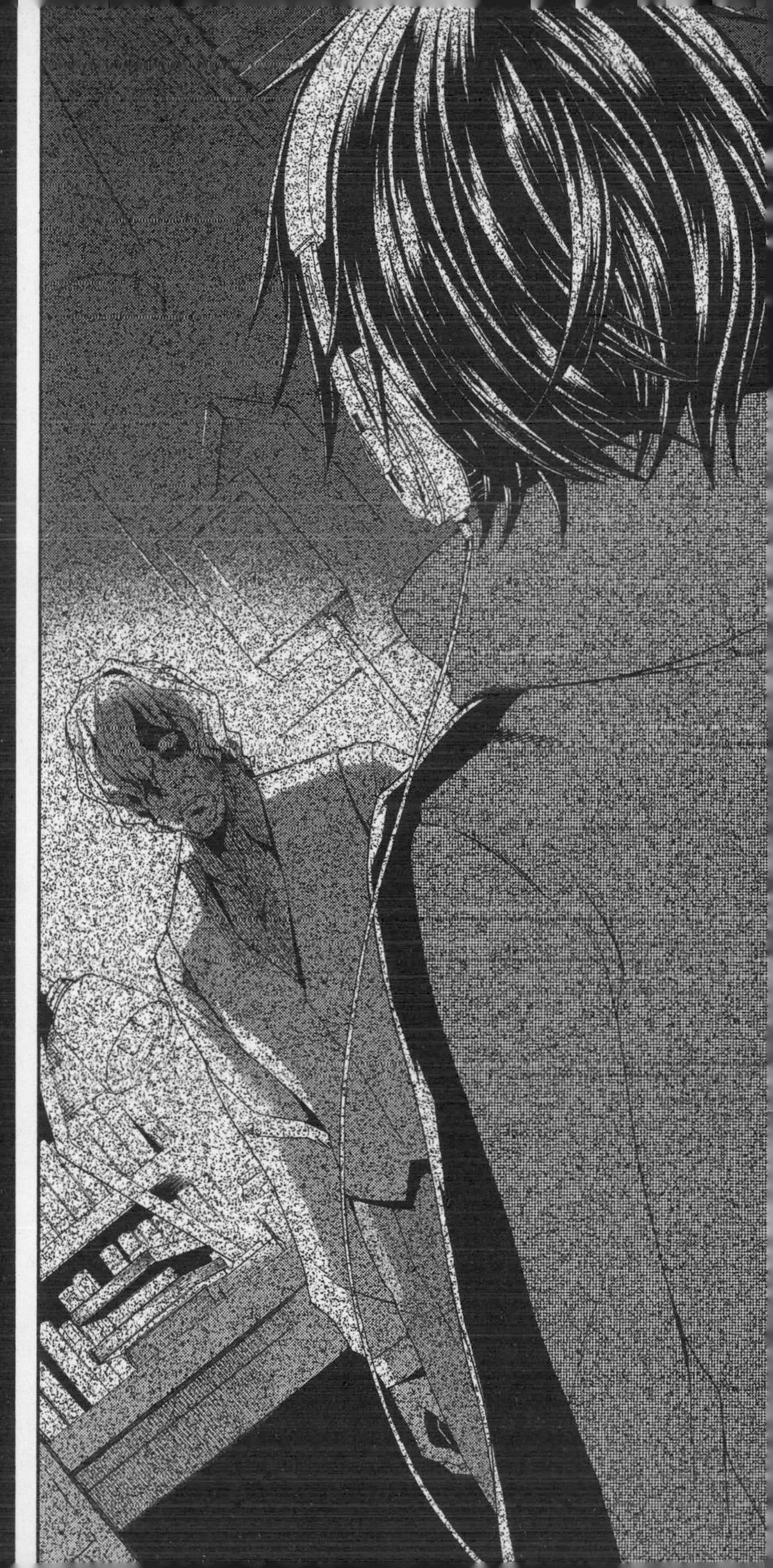

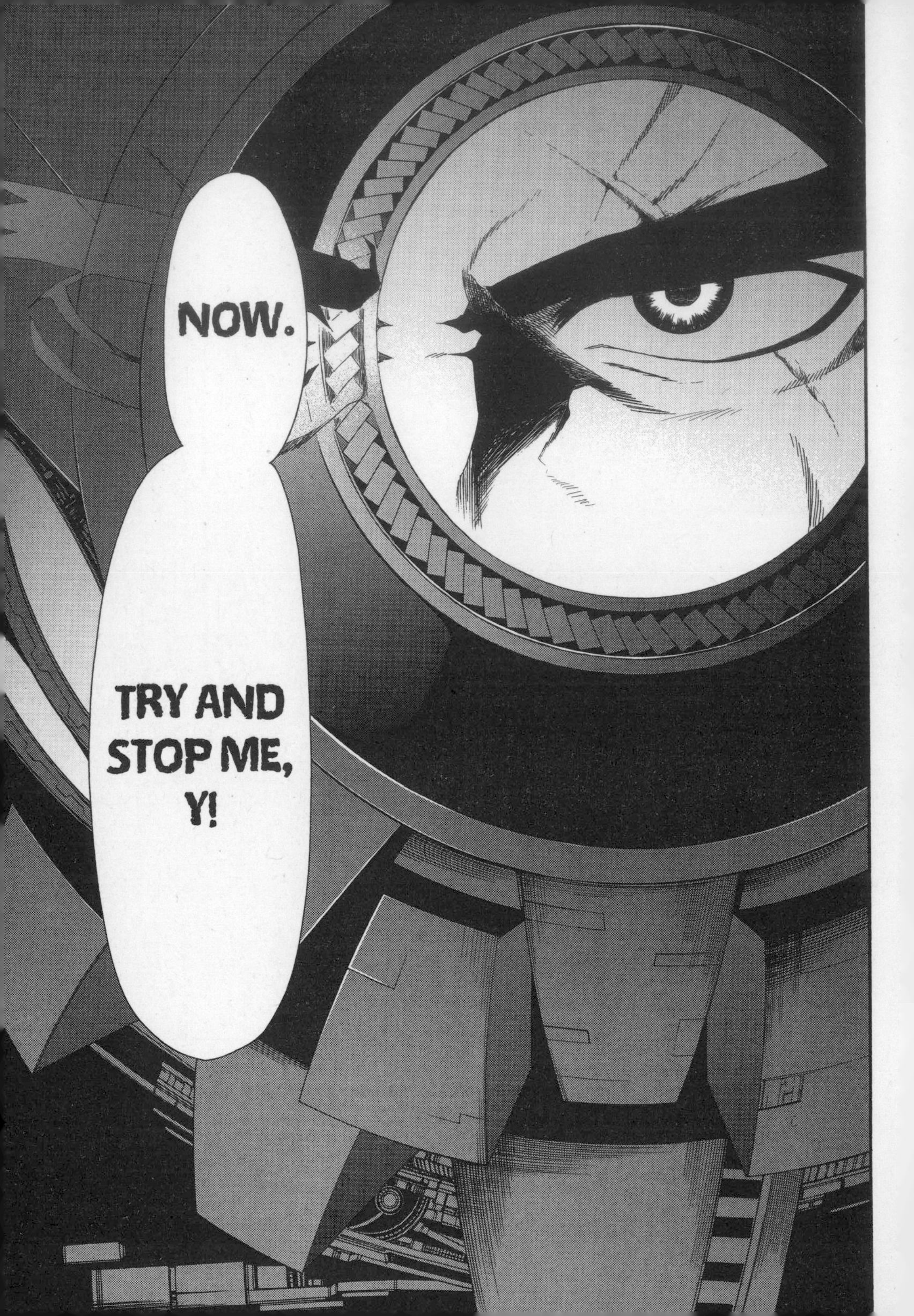
NOW.
TRY AND STOP ME, Y!

IMPERIAL PALACE
ROAR

WHAT A CON-FOUNDING SITUATION THIS CRISIS IS, NO?
THOUGH I AM A WOMAN WITHOUT POWER AT TIMES,
I HOPE THAT YOU WILL LEND ME YOUR AID.
Marie
VI

OH, WHAT WOULD YOU DO TO OVER-COME THIS SITUATION...
...MARIE?
To Be Continued

CLOCKWORK
PLANET

YK: Hey, it just occurred to me, don't you think God exists?

TH: Uh, we're writing the afterword here...but maybe first you should see a doctor. Is your head okay?

YK: Come on, come on, think about it. You and I were both born as humans, the most helpless animals in the natural world, you know? Our parents, their parents, their parents' parents, and so on—they all managed to get through life like that and get you here, you know?! That's why you gotta ask—how is it that humanity still exists?

TH: You sound like you're doing that thing you always do where you suddenly talk as if you're getting serious for once and then—oh, okay. Proceed.

YK: Have you ever seriously thought about the fragility of human life?! Dude, you never know when you could catch a cold and never come back! Who's got time to worry about the pandas and koalas? And they talk about saving the world—who do you think you are? Mother Earth isn't so pathetic she needs friggin' humans to worry about her! You don't need to replace her gears; she'll keep going just fine!

TH: Well, it is true babies come with so many warnings that you ask, "Wait, seriously?"

YK: Right?! So first, let's worry about humans, right?! Humans were born of coincidence? Humans thrived on coincidence? *Ha ha*—yeah, right, like that could ever happen! That's why I'm certain—God clearly exists!

TH: Uh... That's right, I forgot... Congrats, "Daddy." Must be tough raising that kid.

YK: Yeah. Thanks—so, hey, God, could you hurry up and grant me your succor already! (*Kamiya is very tired.*)

TH: But, then, couldn't you also think about it this way? It's because there are no gods that we've managed to survive.

YK: Hmm.

TH: It's because we have no absolute protector like your God that people have had to help and support each other—it's because of that that we discovered love.

YK: Sorry, let me throw this back at you. Is ***your*** head okay?

TH: Look, hear me out. My parents managed to get together, right? And their parents, and their parents... Think about it: None of them are virgins. So maybe you can help me with my great question.

YK: —

TH: If God exists, what the hell is he doing? When's he going to show me my girlfriend? Where is the love?

YK: Uh, yeah...

TH: Therefore, I conclude: There is no God. Humans are alive because they help each other! Love and peace!

YK: I-I see... So what kind of charity have you been performing since you reached enlightenment? Would it be feasible for you to explain?

TH: ...I wonder if you've heard of natural selection? I am contributing to the evolution of humankind by eliminating my genes from the pool in—

YK: Wellll then! We've got an anime on *Clockwork Planet* coming! S-See, Tsubaki? You're getting your debut work made into an anime; miracles do happen! So don't give up! Okay? [Editor's note: the anime has aired as of April 2017.]

TH: So you're saying my passing down my line to future generations is more unlikely than my debut work getting made into an anime... (*Unenthusiastically*) Guess that would be some miracle, ha ha.

YK: Okay! That's all for today, folks! Quitting time!

TH: Where do we come from, and where are we going? (*Eyes vacant*)

YK: (*Hurried*) See you in Volume 6!

Yuu Kamiya & Tsubaki Himana

Afterword

AFTERWORD
ANCLE
I had to talk with my editor for a long time before I figured out how to represent the Mute Scream, but I think it came out okay, and now finally, AnchoR is on the stage after being teased for two volumes. Sino draws girls perfectly, so I've been worried about whether I'm making her cute enough, but she'll continue to be a major player in future developments, so I'll keep doing my best to draw her as cute and mighty as I can!
*ANCLE is the romanization of the Japanese pronunciation of AnchoR's name.
SPECIAL THANKS
☆STAFF / CHIE
/ RIN NEKOYA
☆SUPPORT / MIHO MIYANISHI
☆EDITOR / HIROSHI OGASAWARA
☆DESIGNER / RYO HIIRAGI
(I.W.S DESIGNING)
KURO
2016.3.9

Translation Notes

Yatsukahagi, page 163
In ancient Japan, *yatsukahagi*, literally “eight-bundle shins,” referred to remote Japanese barbarians who refused to serve the emperor. A *tsuka* or “bundle” was the width of the four non-thumb fingers together, implying that they had long shins. It was used as a name for a mythical spider monster. A common synonym for both meanings is *tsuchigumo*, “earth spider.”

Kasumigaseki, page 181
Kasumigaseki is a district of Tokyo, home to Japan's national bureaucracy.

AKIRA

Clockwork Planet volume 5 is a work of fiction. Names, characters, places, and incidents are the products of the author's imagination or are used fictitiously. Any resemblance to actual events, locales, or persons, living or dead, is entirely coincidental.

Published in the United States by Kodansha Comics, an imprint of Kodansha USA Publishing, LLC, New York.

Publication rights for this English edition arranged through Kodansha Ltd, Tokyo.

First published in Japan in 2016 by Kodansha Ltd., Tokyo

ISBN 978-1-63236-466-1

Printed in the United States of America.

www.kodanshacomics.com

9 8 7 6 5 4 3 2 1
Translation: Daniel Komen
Lettering: David Yoo
Editing: Haruko Hashimoto
Kodansha Comics edition cover design by Phil Balsman